The basic-needs approach to development
Some issues regarding concepts and methodology

The basic-needs approach to development

Some issues regarding concepts and methodology

D. P. Ghai
A. R. Khan
E. L. H. Lee
T. Alfthan

International Labour Office   Geneva

Copyright © International Labour Organisation 1977

Publications of the International Labour Office enjoy copyright under Protocol 2 of the Universal Copyright Convention. Nevertheless, short excerpts from them may be reproduced without authorisation, on condition that the source is indicated. For rights of reproduction or translation, application should be made to the Editorial and Translation Branch, International Labour Office, CH-1211 Geneva 22, Switzerland. The International Labour Office welcomes such applications.

ISBN 92-2-101801-6

First published 1977
Third impression 1980

The designations employed in ILO publications, which are in conformity with United Nations practice, and the presentation of material therein do not imply the expression of any opinion whatsoever on the part of the International Labour Office concerning the legal status of any country or territory or of its authorities, or concerning the delimitation of its frontiers.
The responsibility for opinions expressed in signed articles, studies and other contributions rests solely with their authors, and publication does not constitute an endorsement by the International Labour Office of the opinions expressed in them.

ILO publications can be obtained through major booksellers or ILO local offices in many countries, or direct from ILO Publications, International Labour Office, CH-1211 Geneva 22, Switzerland. A catalogue or list of new publications will be sent free of charge from the above address.

Printed in Switzerland

Table of Contents

Preface

Acknowledgements

I.	What is a Basic Needs Approach to Development all About?	D. P. Ghai
II.	On the Principles of Quantifying and Satisfying Basic Needs	D. P. Ghai and T. Alfthan
III.	Some Normative Aspects of a Basic Needs Strategy	E. L. H. Lee
IV.	Basic Needs Targets: An Illustrative Exercise in Identification and Quantification	A. R. Khan
V.	Production Planning For Basic Needs	A. R. Khan

PREFACE

In June 1976 the World Employment Conference proclaimed as a fundamental principle that "Strategies and national development plans should include explicitly as a priority objective the promotion of employment and the satisfaction of the basic needs of each country's population". Basic needs were defined as including, first, certain minimum requirements of a family for private consumption: adequate food, shelter and clothing, as well as certain household equipment and furniture; and, second, essential services provided for and by the community at large, such as safe drinking water, sanitation, public transport and health, educational and cultural facilities. "A basic needs-oriented strategy", the Conference emphasised, "implies the participation of the people in making the decisions which affect them through organisations of their own choice".

The idea of basic needs is by no means completely new. It has evolved out of the growing concern over the recent decades about the increasing poverty and inequality in the Third World. The International Strategy for the Second Development Decade and many subsequent deliberations on the problem at the international forums expressed concern about the problem. The World Employment Conference represents the culmination of such concern through an attempt to dramatise the problem by inscribing the term "basic needs" on the banner of the UN system.

Although the slogan itself has caught on, due largely to the concern about the poor and the poor nations, the clarification of issues and the formulation of an action programme has only just begun. The ILO is devoting significant resources to work on these subjects.

This volume is one of the earlier products of our efforts. It is a collection of essays written by the members of the Rural Employment Policies Branch of the Employment and Development Department. The authors were involved in the methodological work on basic needs that was started after the World Employment Conference, 1976. They were members of a working party that was set up in the autumn of 1976 for this purpose.

The work on the conceptual and methodological problems of quantifying basic needs is by no means complete. The papers in this volume represent some preliminary steps in the direction of clarifying issues. The views expressed do not yet represent the agreed position of the Department or the ILO. Indeed, the readers would discover that the authors of the present studies themselves are not unanimous in their views concerning all the problems.

While the volume does no more than present the first results of the research and conceptual work initiated in the ILO to follow up on the World Employment Conference and lay the basis for implementing its conclusions at the country level, it is hoped that it will generate interest and further discussion. In this way, it will bring us nearer to the identification of the criteria and approaches that should guide our anti-poverty action programme.

Antoinette Béguin
Chief,
Employment and
Development Department.

Acknowledgements

Some of the papers in this volume have drawn on the discussions at various meetings of the Working Party on Basic Needs and our main debt is therefore to Mike Hopkins, Samir Radwan, Guy Standing and Rick Szal, who were members of that Working Party. In addition we wish to thank Enrique Bru, Keith Griffin, Peter Peek, Peter Richards, Hans Singer, Gerry Rodgers, Wouter Van Ginneken and Bob Young, each of whom commented on drafts of at least one of the papers in this volume.

We would also like to thank Pat Carter, Sandra Berlinka, Sheila Finn and Christine Brown for having typed both the draft and the final version of the manuscript under an exacting time constraint.

A Note on the Contents

The reader will find that there are some minor overlaps amongst the five chapters; we do not feel unduly apologetic for this. The subjects treated are all interrelated and a strict compartmentalisation would have been artificial.

The layout of the volume is as follows:

Chapter I serves as a general introduction; it surveys the shifts in development strategies and places the evolution of a basic needs strategy in that context. It then surveys and evaluates the major statements advocating a basic needs strategy of development.

Chapter II is a general synthesis of some of the main issues connected with a basic needs strategy and tries to map out the main lines of conceptual and empirical work that will be required in order to make the strategy operational.

Chapters III - V expand upon and develop some of the issues raised in Chapter II. Chapter III poses some of the main normative issues surrounding the adoption of a basic needs strategy while Chapter IV develops a general methodology for identifying and quantifying basic needs targets and applies it to the case of Bangladesh. Chapter V takes up the problem of production planning for basic needs and shows why a simple reliance on a conventional multi-sector planning model will be inadequate; a basic needs plan will have to take into account the close interrelationship among basic needs targets, the production structure and the distribution of income.

The various chapters were written independently by the respective authors and not as parts of a single piece of work on basic needs. One, therefore, should not expect the unity of thought that characterises a book on some subject. Indeed, as will be apparent, the authors are not quite unanimous on all points.

CHAPTER I

What is a Basic Needs Approach to Development All About ?*
by
D. P. Ghai

I. Introduction

Development fads change with a rapidity equalling if not surpassing the changes in fashions in women's clothing. Leaving aside the many variants of Marxist analysis and prescription for the elimination of "underdevelopment", the last two decades have witnessed a steady stream of the proposed decisive solutions to development problems from the perspective of dominant western schools of thought in social sciences, especially of course in economics. At one time or another, the following have held the centre of the stage in mainstream development economics: capital accumulation; availability of foreign exchange; industrialisation, first of the import substitution variety and then export-oriented; rural development; population control; human resource development; employment-oriented strategies; redistribution with growth - to mention only the star contenders. Whether this profusion of ideas on "how to solve the development problem" is a reflection of poverty of thought on the part of "developmentalists"; a tribute to the fertility of their imagination; the rapidly changing nature of the "development problem" itself, or of some other complex, sociological phenomenon, is in itself a subject of some importance, which, unfortunately, cannot be pursued here.

In the meanwhile, a new fad has been added to the changing kaleidoscope of development concepts, objectives and theories. 'Basic needs approach to development' is the new catchphrase and it seems to be spreading with even more of a lightening speed than its illustrious predecessors. Many questions immediately crowd the

---

* This is the revised version of a paper originally presented at the National Seminar on Employment and Basic Needs in Kenya held at Mombasa in April, 1977.

mind. Is this a slogan devoid of all content? Is it an "approach" or a theory? Does the basic needs approach constitute a strategy for development? If so, what are its key elements and how does it differ from other theories and strategies of development and underdevelopment? It is beyond the scope of this paper to probe all these questions in depth. It has a more limited purpose. In the first place, it seeks to explain the 'appeal' of the basic needs approach. Secondly, an attempt is made to convey some of the flavour of the ideas associated with this approach through an examination of five "statements" on basic needs that have appeared in recent years. Thirdly, some critical comments are made on the adequacy of these statements as outlines of development theories and strategies. Finally, some tentative suggestions are made for future work in this area.

II. Why a Basic Needs Approach?

The fundamental feature of a basic needs approach to development and one which is no doubt responsible for its immediate and widespread appeal is its central emphasis on meeting the basic needs of the poor masses within the shortest possible period. This objective has found a sympathetic response because of the growing disillusionment with the results of the patterns of national and international development over the past quarter of a century. As is well known, this period has been characterised by unprecedented rates of economic growth for the world economy as well as for the developing countries taken as a whole. It is, however, generally accepted that this growth has been very unevenly distributed both within and across nations. In the developing world, only a few countries have been able to pioneer a growth process which has brought substantial benefits to the poor. In the great majority of countries, not only has growth failed to bring about any tangible improvements in the living standards of the poverty groups (usually but often inaccurately defined as the bottom 40 per cent) but it has even often led to their absolute impoverishment[1].

---

[1] For a brief survey of the recent evidence on this case, see K. Griffin and A.R.Khan, "Rural Poverty in Developing Countries: An Analysis of Trends with Special Reference to Contemporary Asia", mimeo. ILO.

All this is well-known and indeed has become part of the conventional wisdom in the "development circles". It is in reaction to this situation that there has been a resurgence of interest in "new development strategies" which emphasise poverty elimination such as employment-oriented strategies, "redistribution with growth", etc. It is not intended in this paper to discuss the content of these strategies and contrast them with the basic needs approach[2]. No doubt there are many common elements in these "new approaches to development" (they are after all not as new as their proponents often claim them to be!) but there are also significant differences. Employment creation is undoubtedly one of the most important instruments for combatting poverty but unless defined in a somewhat special manner, it hardly amounts to a comprehensive strategy for an immediate and direct attack on all forms of poverty[3]. Likewise, redistribution with growth strategies seek to gradually eliminate poverty through marginal transfers of income and assets[4]. The basic needs approach can thus be seen as a logical outgrowth of the "new development strategies", incorporating many of the ideas found there but going beyond them in a number of areas. As shown later, these extensions include the broadening of the concept of development to include so-called non-material needs, the concrete specification of poverty in terms of some core basic needs, the overwhelming priority given to the meeting of basic needs of <u>all</u> families in the shortest time possible, the emphasis on redistribution of income and wealth and the creation of egalitarian societies, the

---

[2] For some of the attempts in this direction, see Franklyn Lisk, "Conventional Development Strategies and Basic Needs Fulfilment", International Labour Review, March-April 1977; P. Streeten and S.J. Burki, "Basic Needs: An Issues Paper" (World Bank, 1977); and Employment, Growth and Basic Needs: A One-World Problem" (ILO, 1976) the Report of the Director-General prepared for the Tripartite World Conference on Employment, Income Distribution and Social Progress and the International Division of Labour.

[3] As a matter of fact, some comprehensive employment strategy missions organised under the World Employment Programme of the ILO have increasingly tended to define "employment problem" to include self-employment, certain minimum income levels for the employed – "productive employment" – and a relatively egalitarian income distribution, e.g. Matching Employment Opportunities and Expectations: a Programme of Action for Ceylon (ILO, 1971) and Employment, Incomes and Equality: a Strategy for Increasing Productive Employment in Kenya (ILO, 1972). Such a definition moves employment-oriented strategies much closer to a basic needs approach but some differences remain.

[4] Hollis Chenery et.al. Redistribution with Growth (London, Oxford University Press, 1974)

key role accorded to public services in combatting poverty and at least some rudimentary analysis of power structures in societies. None of these emphases are of course completely new but the bringing of them all together may perhaps justify the term "basic needs approach to development".

A good deal of the discussion of a basic needs approach thus far has been confined, for the most part, to the national context but such an approach has also potentially far-reaching implications for the structure and growth of the world economy and of the place therein of the developing countries. A basic needs approach with its emphasis on self-reliance; on changes in patterns of demand, consumption and production; on utilisation of local material and human resources to produce goods and services to meet essential needs of the people; on labour-intensive technologies and often small-scale production, has implications for a wide range of international economic issues such as the structure and terms of trade, the transfer of technology, international migration, multinational enterprises and development assistance. A focus on meeting basic needs of the people should imply a lessening of the dependence of the Third World on the markets, capital and technologies of the developed world; a greater potential for trade expansion among developing countries; an improvement in their terms of trade vis-à-vis the industrialised world; a reduced dependence on and role for multinationals and sophisticated technologies; a reorientation of development assistance[5]. All this should reduce the dependence of the developing countries on growth in the industrialised world and in this sense a basic needs approach opens up the possibility of autonomous, self-sustained growth for the Third World which is currently ruled out by their dependent status. The systematic pursuit of a basic needs strategy by developing countries would thus

---

[5] The above statements are merely made here as "assertions". Though they appear to flow from the logic of a basic needs approach, it is necessary to "test" their validity through qualitative and quantitative substantiation. This is indeed one of the important but neglected areas of research.

appear to be a more potent means of realising the Third World demands for a restructuring of the world economy (though not necessarily always in the direction called for under the New International Economic Order) than endless, protracted negotiations.

III. Five Statements on Basic Needs Approach

The question is often asked as to the precise content of a basic needs approach to development. The preceding section has touched upon some of the ideas associated with such an approach. It is, however, necessary now to be more specific on the subject. This task is made difficult by the fact that there is as yet no single document which is generally regarded and accepted as containing a comprehensive and definitive analysis of basic needs concept, objectives and strategy. In the absence of such a "standard source", it is perhaps most useful to look at a number of "international statements" on basic needs that have been made in recent years[6]. An examination of these statements can give a flavour of the main ideas associated with a basic needs approach. For this illustrative purpose, we have selected the following five influential statements: Cocoyoc Declaration; "What Now - Another Development", the 1975 Dag Hammarskjöld Report; ILO's report "Employment, Growth and Basic Needs"; the Bariloche Foundation publication entitled "Catastrophe or New Society? A Latin American World Model"; and the Club of Rome

---

[6] Needless to say development plans and/or policies of several countries have contained for a number of years many of the ideas associated with basic needs approach. And of course there are other international documents such as UNICEF's "Basic Services for Children" (1975) and "Alternative Approaches to Meeting Health Needs in Developing Countries" edited by V. Djukanovic and E.P. Mach, a joint UNICEF/WHO study, (1975), which apply a basic needs approach to their respective areas of concern. Naturally, a more complete paper would have to take account of all such material bearing on basic needs.

report entitled "Reshaping the International Order" (RIO)[7].

Each of these statements was prepared for a special purpose and they therefore differ significantly in scope, approach and objectives, but meeting the basic needs of the poor within the shortest possible period as the central objective of development is a theme common to them all.

The Declaration of Cocoyoc dealt with environment, natural resources, national and international development patterns. On basic needs, the Declaration states:

> "Our first concern is to redefine the whole purpose of development. This should not be to develop things but to develop man. Human beings have basic needs: food, shelter, clothing, health, education. Any process of growth that does not lead to their fulfilment - or, even worse, disrupts them - is a travesty of the idea of development."

And further,

> "Development should not be limited to the satisfaction of basic needs. There are other needs, other goals, and other values. Development includes freedom of expression and impression, the right to give and to receive ideas and stimulus. There is a deep social need to participate in shaping the basis of one's own existence, and to make some contribution to the fashioning of the world's future. Above all, development includes the right to work, by which we mean not simply having a job but finding self-realisation in work, the right not to be alienated through production processes that use human beings simply as tools."

---

[7] The Declaration of Cocoyoc (1974) was a statement issued by a group of social scientists, natural scientists and economists at the end of a seminar organised under the joint auspices of UNCTAD and UNEP on Patterns of Resource Use, Environment and Development Strategies. "What Now - Another Development" (1975) was prepared by a group of individuals on the initiative of the Dag Hammorskjöld Foundation on the occasion of the Seventh Special Session of the United Nations General Assembly. The ILO report (1976) was prepared as the main document for the World Employment Conference of June, 1976. "Catastrophe or New Society? A Latin American World Model"(1976) was prepared by a group of scholars under the auspices of the Bariloche Foundation, Buenos Aires, Argentina, and represents the main results of their on-going work on the project. "Reshaping the International Order"(1976) is the work of an international group of experts working under the leadership of Jan Tinbergen. It was commissioned by the Club of Rome.

The Declaration emphasises the need for diversity and "for pursuing many different roads to development" and it singles out self-reliance as a key element in development. In the words of the Declaration,

> "To arrive at this condition of self-reliance, fundamental economic, social and political changes to the structure of society will often be necessary. Equally necessary is the development of an international system compatible with and capable of supporting moves towards self-reliance."

"What Now - Another Development" also addresses itself to wide-ranging issues in national and international development. The report argues that satisfying basic needs of the poor, identified to include food, habitat, health and education, should be at the core of the development process. At the same time, the report states that:

> "... needs are as much psychological and political as material. To satisfy the latter while forgetting the former would neither be consistent with these values nor indeed possible. However, they form a hierarchy in so far as the satisfaction of survival needs obviously determines the possibility of satisfying the others."

The report spells out in broad terms the kind of changes called for in policies relating to the four needs identified above. As in the Cocoyoc Declaration, the report stresses "endogenous and self-reliant growth" as a key element in "another development". The report then goes on to argue that "another development requires structural transformations". It says the current

> "situation is characterised by:
>
> An international power structure largely based in the market-economy industrialised countries, but organically linked, in a part of the Third World, to local structures, sometimes controlling them directly;
>
> Unequal economic relations, at the international level as well as within the majority of national systems."

The "structural transformations" proposed by the report flow from this analysis. To quote the report again,

> "At the socio-economic level the reform implies ownership or control by the producers - through various institutional forms - of the means of production, i.e. the land, water, mines, infrastructure and factories which supply the necessary goods for production and consumption. Commercial and financial structures must equally be changed in such a manner as to prevent the appropriation of the economic surplus by a minority.
>
> At the political level, the reform of structures means the democratisation of power. It may be necessary first to guarantee concretely the exercise of fundamental rights, in particular the right to express oneself, and the abolition of repression and torture. This is only possible through a thoroughgoing decentralisation, aiming at allowing all those concerned, at every level of society, to exercise all the power of which they are capable."

Among immediate priorities for action, the report stresses the urgency of defining "the needs according to a normative scale, making explicit the desired social values;" establishment of "indicators that assess and monitor the satisfaction of needs by social groups"; identification of "those groups that require immediate and priority action, and to evaluate their needs"; and examination of the "distribution of available resources, the degree to which they are appropriated by certain groups and their relative and absolute over-consumption; and thus to assess the potential of a redistribution policy that, in the short term, scarcity of resources makes unavoidable".

Like the other two documents, "Employment, Growth and Basic Needs" covers a wide field, including development strategies not only in developing countries but in market-economy and socialist industrialised countries, and also some aspects of international economic policies, particularly those relating to adjustment assistance, international manpower movements, technological choice and innovation and multinational enterprises. The central theme running

through the report, however, is the desirability of making the
satisfaction of the basic needs of the poor the central focus for
national and international development efforts. The report goes
considerably beyond the two documents discussed earlier in reviewing
evidence of development over the past quarter of a century, in
identifying and contrasting the key elements of "new development
strategies", and in working out the economic and implementation
aspects of what is described as a basic needs strategy.

Basic needs are defined to include several elements.

"First, they include certain minimum requirements of
a family for private consumption: adequate food,
shelter and clothing are obviously included, as would
be certain household equipment and furniture.

Second, they include essential services provided by
and for the community at large, such as safe drinking
water, sanitation, public transport, and health and
educational facilities.

A basic-needs oriented policy implies the participation
of the people in making the decisions which affect them.
Participation interacts with the two main elements of
a basic-needs strategy. For example, education and good
health will facilitate participation, and participation
in turn will strengthen the claim for the material basic
needs.

The satisfaction of an absolute level of basic needs
as so defined should be placed within a broader framework - namely the fulfilment of basic human rights,
which are not only ends in themselves but also contribute to the attainment of other goals.

In all countries employment enters into a basic-needs
strategy both as a means and as an end. Employment
yields an output. It provides an income to the employed.
And it gives a person the recognition of being engaged
in something worth his while."

The report also considers "making employment more humane and
satisfying ... an element of a basic needs strategy". Furthermore,
"basic needs constitute the minimum objectives of society, not the
full range of desirable attributes, many of which will inevitably
take longer to attain".

The report then reviews the results of some models designed to explore policy alternatives for meeting basic needs over a specified period and concludes:

> "All these calculations, tentative though they be, strongly suggest that in many countries minimum income and standards of living for the poor cannot be achieved, even by the year 2000, without some acceleration of present average rates of growth, accompanied by a number of measures aiming at changing the pattern of growth and use of productive resources by the various income groups; in a number of cases these measures would probably have to include an initial redistribution of resources, in particular, land. The policy package to be adopted will obviously depend on the situation of each country.
>
> To achieve the satisfaction of basic needs within a generation will therefore require action on all fronts, both redistribution and growth together. To be of use, this redistribution must result in the production of more basic goods and services. The provision of adequate employment opportunities is an essential ingredient in this strategy."

The report goes on to spell out the main contours of a basic needs strategy. Key emphasis is placed on reform of price systems; redistribution through asset transfers as well as government taxation and expenditure; decentralisation in decision-making; and appropriate technology. The report also considers the strategic changes called for in the content, organisation and delivery of important public services such as education, health, housing, water supply and environmental sanitation. The implications of a basic needs approach for rural development and industrialisation are outlined. Finally, the report explores some transitional problems as the economy is restructured to meet basic needs, including temporary fall of production in some sectors and rapid increase in demand for essential goods and services. The report recognises the political difficulties in implementing such a strategy and underlines the importance of organising the poverty groups. It states,,

> "It is rarely possible to mount balanced assaults on all goals at the same time. Institutional, financial, political and administrative constraints necessitate

the adoption of a selective approach in using policy
instruments and careful attention to the timing of new
initiatives and programmes. The criteria for choosing
priority tasks at any given time would generally be
that a target is of critical importance, that its attainment is possible, and that the means used will help
resolve subsequent priority problems or at least not
aggravate them. For each criterion, political and administrative as well as economic considerations are important.
For example, agrarian reform is practicable only if political
forces with more strength than those of the landlords can
be mobilised."

"<u>Catastrophe or New Society</u>?" originated as a response to the challenge posed by the Club of Rome publication entitled, "<u>Limits to Growth</u>". The authors of the Latin American World Model set out to disprove the Club of Rome thesis that the exhaustion of natural resources caused by persistent economic and population growth would in the not-too-distant future spell an end to growth. "<u>Catastrophe or New Society</u>?" poses the question: Is it possible to satisfy the basic needs of the world's population without endangering the environment and exhausting global natural and physical resources? Their answer, in a similar vein to that of the Declaration of Cocoyoc and the Dag Hammarskjöld report, is that it is socio-political obstacles and not limitations caused by the scarcity of natural resources that are likely to pose the dominant problems to elimination of poverty. The approach of the Latin American study is to postulate a certain number of basic needs and to demonstrate through a complex mathematical model that these needs can be met for all the inhabitants of the world in a little over a generation and within the constraints of the available natural and physical resources. The model sets specific targets for food, housing and education. In addition, there is an implied target for health, the assumption being that the meeting of basic needs in the former areas is positively correlated with life expectancy. The model shows that if there was complete equality in the distribution of goods and services, the postulated basic needs targets could be attained in the early 1990s in Latin America and in the year 2000 in Africa. Only in Asia would there be difficulty in meeting these targets, and that because of the growing pressure on arable land. All this could be achieved with only moderate rates of economic growth - no higher than those attained in the past[8].

While the model itself is concerned with the demonstration of the physical possibilities of producing enough goods and services to meet specified basic goods for the world as a whole, the authors separately put forward their version of the preferred society in these words:

> "The final goal is an egalitarian society, at both the national and international levels. Its basic principle is the recognition that each human being, simply because of his existence, has inalienable rights regarding the satisfaction of basic needs - nutrition, housing, health, education - that are essential for complete and active incorporation into his culture."

> "The society proposed in the model is not consumer society; production is determined by social needs and not by profit."

The authors go on to say that basic needs are relative, evolve over time and must be determined by the participation of all.

> "Although we assume the free expression of needs and aspirations of each person in the proposed society, decisions are channeled through the mechanism of collective action. This can be developed by starting with those places where individual participation is most feasible, such as in production units of goods and services. Depending upon their significance for the community, issues are discussed, and decisions taken, at different levels in the social and political organisation."

With regard to the ownership of means of production, the authors state:

---

[8] It should be noted that the targets for basic needs are set at relatively high levels in relation to the existing situation e.g. 3000 calories and 100 grams of protein per person per day; 12 years of basic education for all; 7 sq. metres of housing space per person etc.

"It is clear that, in our context, the concept of
property loses much of its meaning. The private
ownership of land and the means of property do not
exist, but on the other hand, neither does the state
own them as is currently the case in many centrally
planned economies.

The present-day concept of private ownership of the
means of production should be replaced by the more
universal concepts of the _use_ and _management_ of the
means of production. How to manage them would be
decided and organised through the same discussion
processes that would regulate all other social
activities. Depending on the nature and importance
of the activity, its management would be the
responsibility of production units, ad hoc committees,
and/or communes of the state.

Within this conceptual framework, many different forms
of management and administration of property will be
found - depending on traditions, cultural features,
and social organisation - that will eliminate property
as a means of achieving power or personal privileges."

As implied by its title, Reshaping the International Order
is an extremely ambitious undertaking. It addresses itself to an
analysis of such major world problems as the armaments race, population, food, environment, natural resources and energy, the oceans
and outer space, and international political and economic institutions and offers proposals for reform. The fundamental aim of the
world community is stated as: "to achieve a life of dignity and
well-being for all world citizens". The "guiding elements" for the
attainment of this aim are listed as equity, freedom, democracy
and participation, solidarity, cultural diversity, and environmental integrity. "The fundamental aim" and "the guiding elements"
should be incorporated in and implemented through "new development
strategies", the main components of which are identified as the
satisfaction of needs, the eradication of poverty, self-reliant
and participatory development, the exercise of public power, and
balanced eco-development.

With respect to the satisfaction of needs, the report says:

"Most of the basic material needs of individuals are concerned
with survival ..... This applies to food and water, health
care and to varying extents, to shelter and clothing".

And again:

> "When bare survival has been guaranteed, the satisfaction derived from labour assumes a more important role. The satisfaction of needs implies that each person available for and willing to work should have an adequately remunerated job ....."

Among the non-material needs, the report singles out education, recreation, leisure and "general socio-cultural activities". In terms of policy areas in new development strategies, the report emphasises the importance of redistributive measures, population planning, adequate food production, land reform, the creation of employment and the provision of education, shelter and public transport.

III. Critical Analysis of a Basic Needs Approach

Before attempting an analysis of basic needs approach as put forward in the above documents, it is important to stress that each of these documents seeks to influence thinking on the broad objectives and directions of development policy. They are not, except perhaps for the Bariloche Foundation study, products of prolonged research. Nor do they contain detailed policy prescriptions. Their purpose essentially is to open up somewhat different perspectives on development problems and sketch out the broad implications of such perspectives.

Some common features of the approaches advocated in these documents may be noted here, though the precise treatment and emphasis put on them varies from one document to another. There is general agreement that the meeting of basic needs of the poor should become the core of development planning and policy. Secondly, basic needs are not confined to only material needs but embrace other dimensions such as fundamental human rights and freedoms, participation, self-reliance, etc. Thirdly, basic needs are not presented in a static manner to be frozen once and for all at fixed levels but as evolving over time in line with the growth of the economy and the aspirations of the people. Fourthly, there is a general consensus that the core material needs should consist of food, education, health and housing and sanitation. Fifthly, there is no single, royal road to achieving basic needs objectives. The

emphasis is rather on diversity and forging of new processes
and institutions in accordance with differing cultural traditions
and other circumstances of individual countries and regions.
Sixthly, all documents stress in varying degrees the need for
"structural transformation", with emphasis especially on
redistribution of assets and incomes. The Bariloche
Foundation and the Dag Hammarskjöld studies stress in
particular the necessity of various kinds of collective
ownership of property and means of production. Lastly,
they all recognise distribution of political power as the central
factor in determining the prospects for the initiation and
implementation of basic needs strategies.

We must now revert to the question posed at the outset
of the paper as to whether the various versions of a basic needs
approach considered above constitute _theories_ of development.
If by theory is meant a body of coherent ideas which explain
the process, pattern and rate of economic development, the
statements reviewed earlier clearly cannot be described as
theories of development. Rather they proceed on the basis of
the acceptance, mostly implicit, of one or other of the existing
theories of development. Can they then be considered as
presenting _strategies_ of development? By strategies is
generally meant the specification of objectives and goals,
the formulation of a set of coherent policy measures, and
elaboration of institutions, processes and instruments for
implementation of policy measures to achieve specified objectives.
Furthermore, there is a growing feeling that a realistic strategy
must systematically incorporate the results of an analysis of the
interaction between alternative policy measures and the
distribution of the political and economic power among
different classes and groups.

The statements discussed here can lay some claim to advancing a strategy of development in the sense considered above. They all specify in more or less detail what should be the fundamental objectives and goals of development policy. They also sketch out in varying degrees of detail the strategic policy changes necessary to attain these goals. In this respect, the ILO report, "Employment, Growth and Basic Needs" goes considerably beyond the others in articulating the required policy changes as well as the means for implementing them. Finally, as indicated earlier, some of these documents contain a rudimentary analysis of the political economy of the proposed policy measures.

However, at their present stage of development, these basic needs approaches suffer from a number of weaknesses. In the first place, they suffer from a failure to integrate systematically analysis and prescription with the underlying political, economic and social forces, both at the national and international levels. With all their emphasis on "structural transformations" and awareness of the importance of political power, they remain largely technocratic exercises. Indeed this is a weakness of all work in "mainstream development economics". It is only works inspired by radical schools of thought which attempt to fuse analysis and prescription for liquidation of underdevelopment with the underlying socio-political and economic forces.

These documents also fail to fully articulate the contours and details required for the formulation and implementation of a strategy. The specification of the objective of satisfying basic needs within the shortest possible period raises some normative and technical issues which must be resolved. These concern, inter alia, the scope of basic needs, the means by which they may be determined, establishment of indicators and targets etc. Some documents such as the ILO report pinpoint the required strategic policy changes but all versions are lacking in a detailed analysis of "how to do it". The sort of questions that one has in mind are: What kinds of institutions are required for the putting into effect of a basic needs strategy? What mechanisms, instruments and measures are needed to bring about the required changes? etc. More generally, there is a need for much more careful and detailed analysis of the problems of transition as economies and societies undergo structural changes of the type postulated in a basic needs approach.

In order to come to grips with these and other weaknesses noted above, it is essential to obtain a much more detailed picture than has so far been attempted of the changes in demand, consumption and production patterns as the economy "shifts gears". Particularly important in this context is an exploration of the production problems and possibilities associated with a radically different demand structure. With appropriate modifications some of the existing planning techniques can serve as useful tools for analysis of these problems.[9] In view of the key role of community services in satisfying some of the core elements of basic needs, it is equally important to work through the problems associated with the design, organisation, content and delivery of services such as health, education, housing and sanitation, transportation, water supplies, etc.

The documents considered above were not of course intended to go into this kind of depth and detail. Much of this sort of work has necessarily to be done in the concrete context of a national setting and hence the importance of country studies. The time has come to move from the generalities to the specifics of a basic needs strategy. This incidentally should also serve to bring into full relief the differences between basic needs approach and other "new development strategies". In the meanwhile, however, there are a number of general issues concerning planning for basic needs which need to be further investigated and clarified. The essays presented in this volume go part of the way in clarifying these issues.

---

[9] For one such useful framework, see Graham Pyatt and Eric Thorbecke, "<u>Planning Techniques for a Better Future</u>" (ILO, 1976).

IV. Conclusion

This paper has attempted to convey a flavour of some of the main ideas associated with a basic needs approach to development. The appeal of this approach lies in its urgent focus on meeting the basic needs of the poor in the shortest time possible. An exploration of this approach leads inevitably to a questioning of many of the features of development patterns pursued in most developing countries and to a search for 'styles of development', institutions, processes, technologies and products which seek in innovative ways to meet the unique problems of the Third World. A systematic pursuit of basic needs policies by poor countries can in and of itself lead over time to major changes in the structural relationships between developing and industrialised countries. Although certain kinds of strategic policy changes are suggested by a basic needs approach, there is as yet no comprehensive, systematic statement of a basic needs strategy, articulating the main contours and details of the range of policy changes required under such an approach. It is necessary now to move from generalities to the specifics of a basic needs approach. This may perhaps be done best by applying such an approach in the concrete context of a national setting.

CHAPTER II

On the Principles of Quantifying and Satisfying Basic Needs

by

D. P. Ghai* and   T. Alfthan**

I. Introduction

This paper is concerned with some conceptual and methodological aspects of defining and quantifying basic needs. These include such issues as the scope and content of basic needs; who should determine these needs and by what processes and means; the indicators to measure basic needs and the principles and techniques of setting targets in respect of these needs. This paper, therefore, covers only a small part - some would say probably the least important part - of what may be described as the basic needs approach to development. A logically prior question is the rationale and justification for a basic needs approach. Other critical questions are the design, content and implementation of a strategy geared to meeting the most important needs of the poor within the shortest period possible. In this connection it is necessary to investigate with some care and depth how a basic needs approach and "strategy" might differ from those generally described as employment-oriented and growth-with-redistribution strategies.[1] While a discussion of the definition and quantification of basic needs cannot naturally be completely divorced from these wider issues, we have attempted - no doubt arbitrarily and not always successfully - to focus our attention as much as possible on developing a framework for analysing methodological questions. This does not mean, of course, that conclusions

---

*   Responsible for Sections I, II, III, IV, VI and VII.

**   Responsible for Section V.

[1] There are, of course, many versions of these latter strategies.

on methodology have no implications for the design, content
and implementation of strategy or that a consideration of the
latter will not in turn call for a revision of the former.
In fact it is our firm conviction that the methodology being
proposed here is merely a first step in a continuing process
of revision and adaptation. This process will be influenced
by both the elaboration of a basic needs strategy and the
experience gained at the country level in applying this
framework. But it is always necessary to make a beginning
and this is the excuse and justification for this attempt.

II. Who Should Determine Basic Needs?

The definition of the scope and content of basic needs
cannot be divorced from the question of by whom and in what
manner these needs are determined. The unequivocal answer
to this is that the people themselves should decide on the
scope, content and priority of their own basic needs. This
is not only consistent with the ethos and spirit of a basic
needs approach founded on self-reliance but any major departure
from it must seem authoritarian, or at best paternalistic.

In what way can people themselves determine their own
needs? In an ideal situation, the people can determine their
own needs <u>directly</u> at the appropriate local units. The
establishment of needs at the national level should then flow
from a consolidation and ordering of needs as reflected
directly by the people at the local level. This will ensure
that the interests and preferences of people, especially the
poor masses, are fully taken into account in determining their
needs. Where direct participation is unfeasible on practical
grounds, <u>representative institutions</u> can perform this function.
These will naturally vary from one country to another and may
consist of political parties, village and town councils,
co-operatives, communes, trade unions and other associations
of various sorts. The important point is that these should be

<u>representative</u> of the people, especially the poorer people, in whose name they speak and the most effective way of ensuring this is through direct and free elections of members of these representative bodies. This presupposes that different groups are adequately organised and possess the necessary educational and material means for giving an effective expression to their interests and preferences. Needless to say, this condition is satisfied in relatively few countries.

The mechanisms and processes by which the people directly or indirectly through their institutions determine their needs raise difficult and complex issues. Apart from the fact that the disadvantaged groups are seldom effectively organised, additional problems are posed by their lack of knowledge of the full range of alternative options and by the constraints they may impose on themselves in expressing their preferences for the quantity and range of basic goods and services they desire. On the other hand, it would be an unnecessarily defeatist and unwarranted position to argue, as some have done, that the scope, content and priorities of basic needs cannot be determined by the people themselves. After all, even more complex issues of political, economic and social policy are often discussed at the local level and consensus reached through discussions and negotiations.

The notion of grass-roots planning is founded on the participation of people in the planning process. It is true that there are not many countries which have succeeded in establishing genuine planning systems based on a grass-roots approach, but this is hardly a reason for questioning the fundamental validity of this approach. This validity derives not only from a rejection of authoritarian and paternalistic alternatives, but also from the inherent strength of participation as a means of articulating genuine needs and satisfying them through self-reliance and mass mobilisation. What is clear is that only limited progress in this difficult area can be achieved by work at the headquarters of an international agency. It is to be hoped that an important

element in the global upsurge of interest in a basic needs
approach to development would be intensified work, at the
national and local levels, in determining the institutions
and processes by which the people themselves can articulate their
own definition and priorities of basic needs.

While determination of basic needs by the people themselves must continue to be a central feature of basic needs
approach to development, realism dictates that acceptance
of this approach at the country level will generally imply
that the process of determining and establishing targets
for basic needs will usually follow the methods evolved
for the formulation of development plans. While there is
considerable country variation in this respect, typically
plan formulation is a highly centralised and technocratic
exercise, with minimal grass-roots participation. It is to
be hoped that acceptance of the basic needs approach will be
accompanied by a progressive increase in the importance of
decentralised and grass-roots planning. But irrespective
of the level at which basic needs are identified and targets
established, a number of conceptual and technical issues arise.
The following discussion is concerned with these issues.

III. The Scope of Basic Needs: Fundamental Human Needs and Rights

The first issue concerns how broadly the concept of
basic needs must be defined. In more specific terms, should
basic needs be defined to include only "material" needs or
should they also comprise in addition more fundamental human
needs and rights? It is tempting to go for the first option.
It can be argued that concentration on material basic needs
provides a focus and "objectivity" to a basic needs strategy
which is lost under the broader definition. In the latter
case, the concept becomes vague, elastic and even more
arbitrary. Furthermore, difficult as it is to get any two
persons to agree on the components of material basic needs,

it becomes virtually impossible to reach consensus on ethical and moral absolutes. Not only do different political, religious and moral systems give different interpretations to fundamental human needs and rights, but the "weight" attached to them varies greatly from one individual to another, even within a given system. Finally, and at a different level, it can be argued that "if some statements about 'human rights' or 'participation' are tagged on to a list of material basic needs such as food and shelter, it could carry several undesirable implications. Ethical absolutes like 'freedom' are treated in the same way as a commodity, thereby giving the impression that it is something to be dispensed with at the discretion of a government. Furthermore, this 'commodity analogy' implies separability between material and non-material needs which is false. The satisfaction of material basic needs is not an end in itself, and, therefore, not separable from how these needs are satisfied."[2] One can no doubt think of other arguments against including fundamental human needs and rights in a listing of basic needs.

Yet the alternative is hardly more appealing. Quite apart from the fact that several of the above objections might with equal force be raised against a more materialistic concept of basic needs, there remains the fundamental point, already hinted above, that satisfaction of material needs can never be accepted without regard to the system and means by which it is brought about. One can envisage situations where material needs can be satisfied in the framework of a highly oppressive and tyrannical régime. There are not many who would accept the meeting of material basic needs at any cost.

---

[2] E.L.H. Lee, Chapter III in this volume.

What then is the way out of this dilemma? Fundamental human needs and rights cannot be treated on par with material basic needs and yet at the same time the materialistic concept of basic needs is seriously deficient. One approach to this issue which suggests itself "would be to preface the discussion of material basic needs with a firm and unequivocal statement of the fundamental values that should form the underpinnings of a basic needs strategy."[3] A statement of this nature should uphold the primacy of certain fundamental human values and rights. "It should also contain within it the notion that these are a pre-requisite to the meeting of basic needs in a more meaningful manner. For example, 'popular participation' is not only desirable [in itself] but is also a highly efficient way of satisfying many basic needs of the people. This would be especially true for community services such as health and education. Innovative ways of meeting these needs through popular participation are likely to ensure greater efficiency, to provide a product more closely related to the needs of the people and also to satisfy, through the production process itself, the goal of popular involvement".[4] More generally, the mass commitment and mobilisation that would appear to be essential in most countries to attain basic needs targets within a reasonable period can only be forthcoming in a system involving mass participation and support.

What then are the fundamental values and rights which should be embodied in a statement of this sort? Evidently human rights and freedoms such as those included in the UN Declaration of Human Rights must figure prominently. In addition, there are certain other values closely linked to a basic needs approach which must be highlighted. The three most important in this context would be the concepts of economic equality, participation and self-reliance. <u>The notion of equality</u> in a sense is central. There are indeed certain

---

[3] E.L.H. Lee, 'Non-material' Basic Needs (mimeo., ILO Geneva.

[4] E.L.H. Lee, ibid.

minimum levels of personal consumption and access to social services which are universally regarded as essential to a decent life. But basic needs are also socially determined and few societies can be content with a situation where the subsistence needs of the masses are met in a context of sharp differences in material welfare and access to communal services. In any case, the majority of the world's poor live in countries so poor that provision of basic needs for the people even at relatively modest levels can only be achieved by much more egalitarian distribution of income, wealth and communal services than is currently the case.

The concept of <u>participation</u> commands widespread agreement, no doubt in large part because it means different things to different persons. It will certainly be necessary at some stage to develop at greater length the precise meaning and implications of a participatory approach in a basic needs strategy. At this stage it is sufficient to state that participation of the entire community in social decisions is an end in itself. It is, however, we believe, also an essential means of attaining basic needs targets in an efficient manner. The discussion above has already hinted at the link between participation, mobilisation and efficiency. In addition to a further investigation of this relationship, a few of the central issues in this area that need to be examined are: what precise meaning must be attached to the notion of participation at different levels of social, political and economic organisation? What does it mean in the context of a village community, a farm, factory, political party, trade union or co-operative? What kinds of decisions must be taken through participation and by what means? Does the notion imply participation of the work force in decisions relating to production and management? Can the question of ownership of means of production be really left out of the picture? Do certain activities and modes of doing things lend themselves more easily to participation than others?

The notion of _self-reliance_ has obvious links with a basic needs approach. In the world as it is, no self-respecting nation or people would wish to see their basic needs met through the charity or whims of the political decisions of foreign nations. Foreign assistance from whatever source has seldom been given out of sheer altruism. More often it has been dictated by the commercial, military and political interests of the "donors" and has sought in various ways to influence if not determine the socio-political and economic policies of the "recipients". In any case, given the realities of the world situation, no feasible amount of resource flows in the foreseeable future are likely to be adequate to meet the basic needs of the masses in the Third World. Self-reliance is thus needed because it is necessary given the realities of the contemporary world situation. In a more fundamental sense, self-reliance as an integral part of a basic needs strategy implies the need to break away from inherited and imposed structures and a search for institutions and processes which seek in innovative ways to meet the unique problems of the Third World. As with participation, the concept of self-reliance raises more questions than can even be enumerated, let alone discussed here. What are the essential characteristics of self-reliance? At what levels and in respect of what should self-reliance be sought? Is it compatible at the national level with extensive economic and other relations with the outside world or parts of it? In what precise ways can the pursuit of a basic needs strategy be expected to lead to reduced dependence on industrialised countries and greater national and collective self-reliance among the Third World countries?

IV. Material Basic Needs

This section is concerned with the components of material basic needs. The next two sections take up the question of indicators and target-setting for basic needs. With respect to basic needs components, one can either work with a fairly extensive list of the items that might enter into a basic needs basket or concentrate on a "core" of basic needs. According to the first approach, a list of basic needs goods and services would be compiled, target levels of consumption would be set in respect of each of these items, and minimum incomes needed to satisfy these needs would be computed from the corresponding price list. The data on a basket of consumption goods are typically derived from household expenditure surveys. It may also be feasible to use other methods such as specialised surveys, or simply discussions with knowledgeable persons, either in conjunction with household expenditure surveys or as substitutes for them, to draw up a list of essential goods and services needed by low-income groups.[5] Such a list might include such components as food, shelter, clothing, water, fuel and lighting, furniture and household equipment, education, health, transportation, contraceptives, recreation and entertainment, social security and so on. The advantage of working with a more or less extensive list is that it brings into its net most of the consumption items of low-income groups. This in turn can provide valuable information for over-all planning in gearing the economy to produce such goods and services. On the other hand, this approach may fail to highlight the critical importance of the more basic of the basic goods and services.

---

[5] For an attempt to derive basic needs basket and income by similar methods, see JASPA reports on Zambia entitled, "Narrowing the Gaps - Planning for Basic Needs and Productive Employment in Zambia"; "Economic Transformation in a Socialist Framework - An Employment and Basic Needs Oriented Development Strategy for Somalia"; "Reducing Dependence - A Strategy for Productive Employment and Development in Swaziland"; and also Richard J. Szal and Rolph van der Hoeven, "Inequality and Basic Needs in Swaziland" (World Employment Programme Research Working Paper, 1976).

The alternative approach of a specification of a core list of basic goods and services has the merit of highlighting deprivation in most critical areas and hence of the need to concentrate efforts on attaining targets in these fields. It has also the advantage of simplicity, is likely to command wider agreement than a more extensive list, and as will be shown later, may have some methodological advantages in setting targets and deriving basic needs income.

Any specification of a bundle of core basic needs must necessarily be arbitrary, in the sense that it cannot be derived from any ultimate, irrefutable principles or system of logic [but then what can]. Furthermore, to repeat the obvious, any such core needs must be country-specific. But the foregoing does not imply either that the concept of core basic needs may not be useful and desirable, or that it is impossible to reach widespread agreement on a small number of items which are meaningful and relevant for the great majority of poor countries. While there are enormous differences of all sorts among developing countries, the poorest groups in them remain deprived of certain goods and services essential for a decent life, even though the degree of deprivation varies from one situation to another. Thus a core bundle of basic goods and services is likely to contain many common elements in practically all poor countries. For our purposes, it is proposed that the following should constitute the core bundle: food, clothing, shelter (including sanitation), health, education and water supply.[6] In many cases, the real issue is likely to be whether this core might be expanded by the inclusion of additional elements such as transportation, fuel and oil, contraception and household furniture and equipment. But at this stage we prefer to work with a smaller core bundle. In the context of a given country, the core could be quite flexible, new items being added and some of the ones included

---

[6] It may be asked why employment is not included as a basic need. The answer is that employment is an essential means to attaining basic needs and must therefore figure prominently in designing a basic needs strategy. It is not necessarily a basic need per se.

in our bundle dropped. It is also essential to add that
basic needs must be seen in a dynamic conte t. Not only
must the target levels go up over time but even the core
components might change in accordance with increasing
incomes and changing preferences.

The level of requirements of basic goods and services,
whether couched in terms of a core bundle or an extensive
list, are inter-related even though in some cases the precise
relationships are not always known. For example, meeting
nutritional needs will have a positive impact on health and
thus reduce the requirements for medical services. Similarly,
shelter, water supply and health are inter-related and
education interacts with other basic needs. These inter-
relationships need to be investigaged and could have a large
favourable impact on the amount of resources needed to
satisfy basic needs in comparison with figures that may be
derived from aggregating independent estimates of the cost
of satisfying each basic need.

Several attempts have been made to categorise the elements
of the bundle in one way or another. One approach is to
order them in hierarchies of importance. This approach is
implicit in the concept of core basic needs. Other
classifications have been suggested such as life-sustaining
needs, life-supporting needs, life-enhancing needs and life-
enriching wants[7]; or deficiency needs, sufficiency needs,
growth needs.[8] A common classification such as was employed
in "Employment, Growth and Basic Needs" divides the bundle
into items of private consumption such as food, clothing
and shelter, and services provided by and for the community
at large, such as safe drinking water, sanitation, public
transport, and health and educational facilities. Others

---

[7] V.T. Vittachi, "A Necessary Utopia", *New Internationalist* September, 1976.

[8] McHale, "Human Requirements, Supply Levels and Outer Bounds", in "*A Framework for Thinking About the Planetary Bargain*" (1975).

have enlarged on this to divide basic needs into three
categories: personal consumption or biological needs,
access to public goods and services, and access to economic
opportunities.[9]

A distinction that comes naturally to persons trained
in neo-classical economic theory is between items of
consumption which yield externalities (positive and negative)
and those which do not.[10] This distinction is exemplified
by that between community services like health and education
and private consumption goods like food and clothing. This
distinction, however, should not be interpreted to mean
that provision of community services confers social benefits
which are lacking in the consumption of private goods:
for surely consumption of adequate food generates wider
social benefits through improved health, productivity etc.,
which may be no less important than those conferred by better
health facilities. It is possible that further work on
categorisation (existing or new ones) may yield useful insights
on basic needs concept. But it is more likely that any
categorisation in the abstract is likely to amount to arid
theorising. The usefulness of any categorisation must
depend on the particular purpose at hand. In this context,
it is not obvious that any of the above categorisations yields
particularly useful insights on the concept of core basic needs.
However, the distinction between goods of personal consumption
and community services is a simple one and has a common-sense
appeal. Likewise, the concept of externality-generating goods
and services will be found useful in further analysis of
quantification of basic needs.

---

[9] Franklyn Lisk and Diane Werneke, "Alternative Development Strategies and Basic Needs"(World Employment Programme Research Working Paper, ILO, 1976).

[10] The reference made earlier to inter-relationships between various basic needs is a particular instance of this more general point.

V. Indicators of Basic Needs

The previous section was concerned with defining a core bundle of basic goods and services. In this section we shall be primarily concerned with the statistical requirements for defining basic needs with respect to these commodities, for measuring current shortfalls from target levels of satisfaction, and for monitoring progress towards meeting basic needs targets. We shall survey the existing statistical sources and evaluate their suitability for use within the context of planning for basic needs.

The existing information falls into three categories viz: (i) definitions of minimum requirements (e.g. of food requirements, of the content of education, etc.); (ii) data on the pattern of consumption of (and access to) a particular good or service at a point in time; (iii) data on the supply/availability of a particular good or service at a point in time. These data can be used in various ways: (a) the definition of minimum requirements can in some circumstances be used as **targets** where a country chooses to set its basic needs targets at minimum levels; (b) comparing (ii) with (i) will generate information on **shortfalls** of basic needs satisfaction in relation to minimum requirements; (c) the data in (iii) can be used to estimate required increases in supplies of certain goods and services in order to meet minimum requirements defined in (i).

For want of a better term, we shall refer to these data as **indicators** of basic needs, with 'basic needs' in this particular usage serving as a general term incorporating the notions of minimum requirements, targets, shortfalls from basic needs targets, etc.

There is a vast literature on indicators represented by the work of UNRISD, WHO, FAO, UNESCO and others over a number of years. This is clearly a field calling for intensive, multidisciplinary work. All that is attempted here is to put

forward some simple, workable criteria for measuring core
needs. Clearly a great deal of further work is required
in refining these measures. But it is important not to
devote excessive amount of time to development of ever more
sophisticated indicators. This would be to lose sight of
the main purpose behind this exercise. To the extent
possible, one should aim at developing indicators which are
easy to construct; are readily comprehensible; draw upon
data already available in one form or another; lend themselves
to the building up of distributional profiles and are not just
national averages; readily measure access and usage; and at
the same time capture how adequately particular needs are
being met. This may be asking too much of a single or a
small group of indicators of basic needs. But to the extent
possible, it is these criteria which must serve as paramount
guides in our search for appropriate indicators. While
there is some existing information on basic needs indicators,
it is clear that in certain areas and for certain countries,
it will be essential to generate the required information
through a variety of methods.

Food

The first item of basic needs which in most poor
countries could also be designed as the __dominant__ item is food.
An "ideal" target would be to have a level and content of
nutrition that satisfies all kinds of requirements (e.g.
calories, proteins, vitamins and other vital nutrients) and
which would be reasonably consistent with consumers' preferences.
However, it has been observed that when energy requirements are
satisfied, protein deficiency rarely occurs. Non-calorie/
protein (including vitamins etc.) could be largely supplied by
special tablet/powder programmes which are cheap and could be
included among publicly provided goods. One suggestion would,
therefore, be to use the calorie measure alone as an indicator
because of its simplicity.

We might mention here that UNRISD in its work on social indicators and in its attempts to define an Index of the Levels of Living used three <u>indicators</u> by which the component of nutrition was measured. The indicators used were:

(i) number of calories absorbed per person per day;
(ii) quantity of proteins absorbed;
(iii) percentage of calories emanating from cereals, roots, tubers and sugars.

When estimating the degree of satisfaction of this need the calorie indicator is given more weight than the other two. The third indicator (iii) is an indirect indicator which aims to estimate deficiencies in the intake of vitamins and minerals. Direct measurement of the absorption of vitamins and minerals is very difficult and costly to perform.

The FAO tie their definition of food requirements to a reference man who is 20-39 years old, weighs 65 Kg and is involved in moderate work for eight hours a day. The standard requirement is 3,000 K calories and 17 grammes of protein per day. The figures are adjusted for sex, type of activity, age and body weight, but no adjustments are made for climate. National averages of calorie and protein requirements are calculated by relating national characteristics to the reference man.[11]

Obviously we would have to relate the per capita calorie requirements to the amount and kind of labour an individual or a household is involved in. The majority of the poorest income groups in many developing countries are often engaged in heavy manual work. Instead of using average calorie requirements, we have to evaluate the additional calories required by those doing heavy work. Assuming a certain ratio between earners (= heavy workers) and the rest of the household,

---

[11] M. Hopkins, "Basic Needs Approach to Development Planning - A View" (World Employment Programme Research Working Paper, 1977).

we could estimate the total calorie requirements of a household.[12] If the sectoral pattern of employment is varied and there are differences in work load, further measurements of additional calorie requirements would be called for. Involuntary unemployment should not, however, be used as an argument for lower calorie requirements.

As to the **measurement of shortfalls** in meeting nutrition requirements, we note that nationwide deficiencies are relatively easy to measure whereas the deficiencies at the micro or household level pose difficult problems. What we need are household consumption surveys to map the extent and nature of shortfalls. Careful design of such surveys is vital since household food consumption varies from day to day, week to week and season to season. Other measurement problems are connected with the distribution of food within the family; this could be unequal with women and children suffering in favour of the male income earners. The surveys must analyse the information both within and between households. They must be comprehensive so as to aid the analysis of why there are shortfalls.

For newly born infants and children at pre-school and school age another method could be used to estimate whether basic food requirements are being met or not. By measuring birth weight and weights at given height and ages, to mention a few of such measures, we can arrive at indicators showing the nutritional status of the child. If these measurements are related to certain standards (targets) we would get information on whether, and to what extent food (and health) requirements of pregnant women, infants and children are being satisfied. These measurements are easy and cheap to make. This point is taken up further in the section on health.

---

[12] A.R. Khan, Chapter IV in this volume.

Clothing

Clothing should give <u>physical protection</u> against the elements and satisfy the cultural needs of the population. UNRISD in its research on indicators for measuring the level of living considers clothing needs to be basically culturally determined. Opting for a basic needs strategy however implies that the economic, social and attitudinal structures of society may have to change. This point is developed at greater length in the section on target-setting. Thus, the cultural standards in clothing should be regarded as changeable, not immutable. The following factors should be taken into account when estimating clothing needs:

(a) climatic conditions (disaggregating needs according to climatic regions within a country);

(b) the type of work being performed which determines the wear and tear (disaggregation by occupational groups);

(c) local customs which determine standards of public decency or some other relative cultural standard (disaggregation according to, say, ethnic origin).

The concept of a "standard of public decency"[13] could be used to indicate the ingredients of clothing that are regarded as absolutely necessary to preserve decency (especially for women to appear publicly). Hence, the decency requirements in metres of cloth and number of shoes per household could be estimated and compared with the actual consumption of cloth and footwear of households. From household expenditure surveys, we could arrive at a measure of the number of households which do not have their clothing requirements satisfied.

Another criterion would be to estimate clothing needs according to the occupational group which the head of the household belongs to. This would require interviews and observation aimed at finding out the basic clothing requirements for each type and intensity of work. In some countries climatic conditions could be a main determinant for clothing needs.

---

[13] A.R. Khan, Chapter IV in this volume.

Which of these determinants for clothing needs to choose would obviously depend on local conditions and would have to be decided case by case. In some circumstances all three criteria mentioned above have a bearing on clothing needs; in other cases only one criterion could prove sufficient for determining the need.

Shelter

UNRISD[14] uses three indicators for measuring the adequacy of housing facilities:

(a) the importance of the services provided by a house: according to the quality of the house;

(b) density of occupation: number of persons per room;

(c) "independence of the user": relationship between number of housing units and the number of household units.

More wight is given to indicator (a) which is <u>qualitative</u>.

The UN World Housing Survey in 1974 came to the conclusion that in developing countries the housing shortage is not quantitative but qualitative. The majority of these countries are able to accommodate their inhabitants in the existing housing stock at a rate of between 1 and 1.5 households per unit. Available information indicates that "the stock is composed of a high percentage of housing units which are marginal and others which are unfit for habitation". To measure quality the UN suggests as an indicator percentage distribution of households and persons according to availability of water supply, toilet, lighting, cooking and bathing facilities.

It is very difficult to specify the required quality of a house since local conditions in terms of climate, construction materials used, design of house etc., vary widely. The only specification one can make is to say that the house should give adequate protection against rain, storm and winter air, and provide access to reasonable toilet facilities.

---

[14] UNRISD: <u>Index of the Level of Living</u>; Report No. 4, Geneva, September 1966.

As to the quantitative indicators, we could use <u>number of persons per room</u> or <u>square metres per room or housing unit</u>. Again quantitative targets must be decided locally. Using the qualitative indicators mentioned above which indicate <u>protection against exposure</u> together with certain quantitative indicators, it should be possible to estimate <u>the quantities of housing materials required</u> as inputs for improving existing houses and building new ones so that they would satisfy housing needs.

To achieve the basic housing targets, there must first be guarantee of access to the piece of land on which the house will be erected. Access to housing land will often have to be provided by changes in the legal and institutional framework of society. The next step would be to develop ideas about sanitation, for example, how to set up simple but hygienic toilet facilities and how to design houses.[15]

Health

The basic purpose of health services is to ensure a certain life expectancy, to eliminate mass diseases and to provide for medical facilities in case of disease and ill-health. A measure of the need for health services (as well as of the need for other components of basic needs goods and services, like food, education, sanitation) is provided by:

(a) indicators on the actual health of population such as:
   (i) age-specific mortality and morbidity rates;
   (ii) rate of deaths due to infectious and parasitic diseases;

(b) incidence of infectious and parasitic diseases;

(c) expectation of life at birth.

---

[15] A.R. Khan, op. cit.

One constraint in using these indicators is the shortage of data. Generally, we have aggregate figures (a single national figure for the variable) but no figures on the distribution according to sex, age, social classes, regions.[16]

Mortality and morbidity are difficult and costly to measure, especially when levels are high. Mortality rates are also not very specific as a health measure since they do not indicate the causes of mortality.

To use indicators of the above type for measuring how basic health needs are satisfied would often imply a gigantic and costly data collection effort, especially if we want to have data on the distribution between different social groups.

Another set of indicators are those measuring certain physical characteristics, generally of children at different stages of their development. As perceived in the WHO nutritional surveillance system[17], a change in an indicator, say **weight for age**, is a reliable signal for action, only if the change or trend is outside the range of normal or usual variation. The table below shows an abbreviated list of indicators of nutritional status.

---

[16] See UNRISD Research Data Bank of Development Indicators.

[17] Methodology of Nutritional Surveillance, Technical Report Series 593, WHO, Geneva, 1976.

Abbreviated List of Indicators of Nutritional Status

Phenomenon	Indicator
Maternal nutrition	birth weight
Infant and preschool child	proportion being breast fed and proportion on weaning foods, by age in months
	mortality rates in children aged 1, 2, 3, and 4 years, with emphasis on 2 year-olds
	If age known: weight for height height for age weight for age
	If age unknown: weight for height arm circumference clinical sign and syndromes
Schoolchild nutrition	height for age, and weight for height at 7 years or school admission
	clinical signs

This set of indicators could also be included in our group of indicators for measuring satisfaction of basic food needs.

WHO suggests the use of so-called "cut-off points" and "trigger levels" to initiate intervention. Suppose the indicator is the proportion of children below 70 per cent of expected weight for age. Here the value of 70 per cent weight for age has been chosen as a "cut-off point". A decision to act might be taken when the proportion of children with weight for age below that value is, for example, 10 per cent, this figure being chosen as the "trigger" level. It is essential to know the distribution of any given measurement in order to be able to define the values that trigger action.

Indicators such as <u>weight for age</u>, <u>height for age</u>, etc., reflecting growth deficiencies resulting from under-nutrition and infections can be very useful since they are easy and cheap to construct.

A third set of indicators relate to the adequacy of existing health services. These show quantities of physical or human capital available or employed in health and medical services, for example, inhabitants per physician, nurse and midwife; inhabitants per hospital bed. Compared with our first set of indicators, data availability is fairly good. For 1970 the number of countries with data on inhabitants per physician numbered 107.[18]

It should be easy to arrive at similar figures disaggregated by region. These variables could be used as complementary indicators when measuring the satisfaction of basic health needs, since they describe some of the <u>necessary</u> but not sufficient material and human inputs in basic health services. They do not show how basic health needs are actually satisfied. A low rate of inhabitants per physician or inhabitants per bed does not indicate to what extent the poorer or regionally remote sections of the population have access to or really make use of such services. However, there must be some <u>reasonable target</u> or <u>critical figure</u> of inhabitants per physician, or per hospital bed above which basic services are not available and thus basic health needs remain unsatisfied.

The principal requirement of healthy growth and development is good nutrition. Here, our indicators mentioned in the section on food are relevant as well as those mentioned below for measuring nutritional status of children.

Closely related to this is the requirement for measures to improve the state of affairs described by indicators relating to percentage of deaths due to infectious and parasitic diseases and incidence of such diseases. To do this

---

[18] UNRISD <u>Research Data Bank of Development Indicators</u>, Vol. 1.

is however more a question of improving the physical and social environment rather than purely a matter of providing medical and health services.

The next target in health should be to provide adequate attention in the case of illness, child birth and infant care. One indicator on the access to such medical and health attention is to specify a minimum target ratio of population to medical worker, disaggregated perhaps by regions. The work of such medical workers should be multi-purpose, providing advice and assistance in fields such as health, nutrition, education and sanitation. For example, they should be able to:

(a) perform preventive health measures, say administering immunization against certain diseases;
(b) supervise collection, treatment and storage of human excreta for utilisation as fertilizer; organise campaigns against pests;
(c) perform some simple curative services or treat light diseases such as minor ailments, gastro-intestinal illness, colds and bronchitis;
(d) perform services for child care and child births;
(e) advise on use of contraceptives.

In both health and education (see below) <u>geographical access</u> to these services can be measured by locating "the service points" (say schools and medical workers) on a map.[19] With an assumption of an area of coverage, e.g. a diameter of x kilometres, the existing facilities can be encircled to see what proportion of a country is covered. With the additional help of a population density map the proportion of the population uncovered by these circles can be estimated. This proportion would be an access indicator.

---

[19] On the methodology for measuring access to health and education services, see Szal and Rolph van den Hoeven: op. cit.

Education

Education should provide the necessary tools which enable an individual to participate fully in society. At the same time, education is a basic need per se, and can thus be viewed as an end in itself.

Although physical and social environments differ widely between (and within) countries we could conceive of a certain minimum package of essential learning needs which must be satisfied to enable people to participate **effectively in** society. We could as an example have six elements of a minimum package of basic learning requirements[20] (intended for rural children):

(a) positive attitudes towards co-operation with and help to family and fellow men, toward work, community and national development, toward continued learning and toward development of ethical values;

(b) functional literacy and numeracy sufficient (i) to read with comprehension a national newspaper or magazine, useful agricultural, health, and other how-to-do-it bulletins; (ii) to write a legible letter to, for example, a friend or to a government bureau requesting information; and (iii) handle important common computations - such as measurement of land and buildings, calculation of agricultural input costs and revenues, interest charges on credit and rental rates on land;

(c) a scientific outlook and an elementary understanding of the processes of nature in the particular area as they pertain to say health and sanitation, to raising crops and animals, to nutrition, food storage and preparation and to the environment and its protection;

---

[20] We have taken this illustrative example from **Philip H. Coombs et. al.** : New Paths to Learning for Rural Children and Youth, (New York, 1973).

(d) functional knowledge and skills for raising a family and operating a household, including elements such as protecting family health, family planning, good child care, nutrition and sanitation; cultural activities and recreation, care of the injured and sick, intelligent shopping and use of money, making clothes and other consumption goods, house repairs, and environmental improvements, growing and preserving food for family consumption;

(e) functional knowledge and skills for earning a living, including not only skills required for a particular occupation but also knowledge of a variety of locally useful common skills for agriculture and non-farm use;

(f) functional knowledge and skills for civic participation, including some knowledge of national and local history and ideology, and understanding of one's society; awareness of government structure and functions; taxes and public expenditures; available social services; rights and obligations of individual citizens; principles, aims and functioning of co-operatives and of local voluntary associations.

The indicators for measuring the quantity and the quality of education are not easily determined. First, we could conceive of indicators which estimate the _inputs_ used in the educational system, say number of students per teacher and classroom, or dollars invested per student. In this group we would include enrollment rates as well since these rates are a function of the material and human inputs in the educational system. Second we could arrive at a measure of the quantity of education received through indicators on the educational process itself, an example being number of years of schooling. Third, we could use as educational indicators the results of education received, say as conceived in our six educational elements above.

The first two sets of indicators are quantitative, but at the same time give some very rough indication of the quality

of education. Enrollment rates in basic education can be
useful in showing quantitative trends, but are often
considerably inflated as for example older children are
included in enrollment rates for the group of 6 to 12
year old children. Thus, enrollment rates can exceed 100
per cent. Educational indicators such as these can be used
as supplementary aids in measuring how basic education is
being satisfied. To get to the root of measuring whether
basic education needs are met or not, we have to develop
indicators showing the _results_ of education received, or in
other words develop techniques for _evaluating_ basic education
programmes. The obvious indicator for measuring how (part of)
element (b) of our basic learning needs is satisfied is the
literacy rate, which should be supplemented by a "numeracy
rate". For the other elements a range of _attitudinal_,
cognitive and _skill_ indicators have to be developed for
testing how education needs are being satisfied. Such
tests could consequently be used in evaluating education
programmes, for example by "tracing up" students who have
received basic education.

We could also use indirect methods to indicate how
educational needs are being satisfied. As to the working
skill component, supplementary indirect indicators that could
be used would be manpower shortages, unemployment and under-
employment rates. These direct and indirect indicators on
satisfaction of basic education needs could be supplemented
by our first set of indicators mentioned earlier to form a
package for evaluating basic education. Access to education
in geographical terms can be measured as was suggested in the
section on health.

Water and Sanitation

Clean water is required for drinking, for maintaining a
sanitary environment, to keep food clean and for practising
good personal hygiene. As water is provided more or less
directly by nature, the access to and use of it will be

strongly dependent upon local conditions, since the supply of groundwater, surface water and rainwater varies widely between countries and regions.

The obvious indicator is to have an assessment of the proportion of households which have reasonable access to clean water. In the World Housing Survey, the Centre for Housing, Building and Planning of the Department of Economic and Social Affairs of the UN Secretariat used as an indicator the "percentage of occupied dwellings with piped water inside or outside the dwelling but within 100 metres". Again the exact target in terms of distance has to be defined case by case according to feasibility.

However, in densely populated areas this access indicator would possibly not be sufficient since every household would daily need a certain time for making use of a tubewell. It has been suggested that approximately 45 minutes use of a tubewell by each household in Bangladesh would be necessary to satisfy its water needs.[21] Thus, in short, we would have two indicators, one indicating access in distance terms and one indicator showing numbers of households to be served per tubewell.

A related field is the sanitary facilities, which have a clear impact on health and hence on the need for health services. The Housing Survey uses "percentage of occupied dwellings with toilet". In many countries this might prove an irrelevant indicator, especially in rural areas. Number of persons served by a latrine might prove more operational in rural areas.

---

[21] A.R. Khan, op. cit.

VI. Setting Targets for Basic Needs

The preceding discussion has been concerned with selecting appropriate indicators for the core bundle of basic needs. The next issue concerns the establishment of targets for basic needs. In this section, we therefore discuss the desirability of setting targets; the geographical level at which they might be set; the relationship between basic needs targets and poverty lines; and the level, sequence and time frame in the establishment of such targets.

The first question - perhaps a rhetorical one - is: should targets be set at all? The selection of appropriate indicators and information on the distribution of consumption of basic goods and services among the population will only give us "profiles of basic needs satisfaction" in each country. Targets for core bundle need to be set in order to give direction to the entire development effort - both at national and international levels - and to evaluate progress in the implementation of a basic needs strategy. At what level should these targets be set? They should obviously be set at the national level, but in addition most countries may find it useful to set them at regional and local levels as well to allow for diversity and for special problems of some regions. It may indeed prove necessary to set different types of targets at least in respect of some basic needs for rural and urban areas. Conditions of work and even styles of living vary enormously in the countryside and crowded cities. Housing and sanitation are obvious examples which require different treatment in rural and urban areas. It is important to stress that such differential targets should not support and perpetuate rural/urban inequalities. The point that is being made here is that different physical and living environments may require different types of target for different regions of the country.[22]

---

[22] For more detailed discussion of this at the level of concrete target-setting, see Szal and van der Hoeven, op.cit.

Should targets also be set at the international level? One can think of several plausible arguments against this and there is no doubt that the idea of universal targets for core basic needs has not aroused much enthusiasm. But there are some compelling arguments to the contrary and it will be a great mistake to abandon the idea. Just as the ultimate objective of national targets is to ensure that every person and household enjoys a certain minimum consumption standard over a specified period, likewise the objective of universal targets is to ensure that no household at a global level falls below a certain minimum consumption level. A commitment to such targets expresses clearly global responsibility for ensuring the meeting of core basic needs for every family in the world. Thereby, it gives a concrete focus and purpose to international development efforts and provides a compelling criterion for evaluating international economic and social policies. The form these targets might take and the level at which they should be established, are questions which deserve a study in their own right, particularly in the context of preparations for the next Development Decade Strategy. Differences in climate, social customs and institutions can be adjusted for. In principle, there does not appear to be any reason for not advancing beyond national to universal basic needs targets.

Reverting to national target-setting, one issue that one faces immediately is the form that these targets might take. As stated earlier, one possible approach is to fix the targets for core basic needs in physical terms in accordance with the indicators discussed above. It may well be that in certain countries this approach will prove adequate, at least in the early stages of planning for basic needs. It has the virtue of simplicity. It calls for concentration of all development efforts to meet the most basic of the basic needs. It may further be argued that once these targets are achieved, others may automatically be realised. However, while adequate in certain circumstances,

this is clearly not a fully satisfactory approach. The
normal consumption pattern of even the poorest groups is
not confined to the core bundle. In order to assure
consumption of other goods and services, households must
dispose of an adequate income.

At this stage, it is useful to make the distinction
referred to earlier between private and public consumption
goods and services. The precise specification of items
falling in each of these categories no doubt varies
considerably from one country to another and within one
country over time. Furthermore, many items may fall in
both the categories simultaneously in a country at any
given time e.g. education and health may be purchased
privately or provided free of charge or on a subsidised basis
by the state. Likewise while most households will purchase
foodstuffs in the "market", there may be special food
programmes handled directly by the state. While taking
account of these qualifications, it is nevertheless useful
for methodological purposes to make the distinction between
private and public consumption goods and services.

The poverty line approach seeks to estimate an
income which will assure a certain minimum private consumption
of goods and services for poor households. The data on a
basket of consumption goods are typically derived from
household expenditures surveys. Given the information
on prices and target levels of consumption, these surveys
can be utilised to readily yield a basic needs income
figure.

There are several possible advantages of this approach
which should be recognised. In the first place, by
definition, income targets are set at a level to permit
consumption of basic needs goods and services. Secondly,
this approach preserves the principle of consumer sovereignty
as revealed through actual household expenditures patterns.

In other words, the bundle of goods and services constituting the basic needs of poor people are not handed down from above or decided in a paternalistic manner, but to the extent possible, are based on preferences expressed by them through their actual expenditure. Thirdly, the approach has the advantage of familiarity and operational ease. Most countries have experimented in one form or another with the computation of poverty lines. In some, these are fairly sophisticated and broadly approximate the level of real income which if attained by all households would remove the worse deprivations caused by poverty. In other countries which lack the data for computing such poverty lines, minimum urban and rural wages may be appropriately adjusted to move them nearer to the concept of poverty lines. The operational advantages of this approach are that the required data are generally available or can be readily generated according to a known and tested methodology, and poverty lines are therefore convenient instruments for measuring deprivation of basic needs and evaluating progress in attaining targets.

In its simplistic form, this approach also suffers from a number of drawbacks. The alleged strength of this approach lies in its grounding in household expenditure surveys. Yet those surveys suffer from a number of deficiencies. They reflect, as they must, the existing inter-related patterns of prices, income distribution and demonstration effects. It is clear that if there were substantial changes in income distribution, as would be called for in meeting the basic needs of the people within a reasonable time frame, the pattern of prices and consumption expenditures would change correspondingly. In a situation of this sort, the consumer sovereignty as reflected in household expenditure patterns may be illusory, and such surveys by themselves cannot serve as infallible guides. Secondly, the poverty line approach, at any rate in its simple form, makes no allowance for social benefits and costs in consumption of goods and services. This argument is particularly valid in the context of community services like health, education, sanitation, etc., but may also be applicable in varying forms to amount and pattern of expenditure on items like food. Household budget surveys merely record private expenditure on items like health, education, etc., but given the fact that many of such services are provided in varying degrees by the public sector either freely or on a subsidised basis, reliance on such surveys to derive a poverty line which allows for adequate absorption of such services can be seriously misleading. Finally, the poverty line approach focussing as it does on a single income figure fails to highlight the critical importance of the more basic of the basic goods and services. There is a danger that one of the main values of a basic needs approach - focussing of attention on deprivation by vast majorities of the most fundamental requirements for a decent life - may be obscured or lost in the mystique of a single income figure.

A related approach but one founded firmly on basic needs is to estimate what may be called basic needs income (BNI)[23] on the basis of stipulated levels of consumption of a few items of the core bundle. This income will be needed to implement the private consumption part of the basic needs programme. It may be estimated on the basis of the required level of the dominant item of basic need e.g. food, or of a small core such as food, clothing and shelter. There are arguments against relying on a single dominant item like food.[24] Reliance on a small core of basic needs - say food, clothing, shelter - is likely to yield more satisfactory results.

---

[23] This terminology is due to A.R. Khan, op.cit. The methodology to determine BNI from core bundle was also developed by Khan in this paper.

[24] Khan, ibid.

Having agreed on the stipulated levels of consumption of the core bundle, one would still need to rely on some sort of household expenditure surveys to generate BNI. The procedure would be as follows: one would identify the marginal household which absorbs the stipulated quantities of the three core items. The total expenditure of this household would then yield the required BNI. Needless to say, ideally it would be necessary to adjust this figure for the size and composition of the household.

The next question is how to overcome some of the deficiencies associated with reliance on such surveys. The first problem concerns goods and services which are included in the private consumption basket but have externality characteristics i.e. they yield social benefits and costs different from the private ones. To get round this problem, it would be necessary to identify such goods and services and ensure their adequate absorption by one or a combination of the following methods: adjustment of BNI through revision of required quantities of consumption (already taken care of for core goods), use of appropriate taxes and subsidies, or direct provision of such goods and services by the state to correct for deficit or surplus consumption.

The second problem arises from the fact that the current relative prices reflect existing patterns of income distribution and production. Redistribution of income and wealth that would be necessary in a basic needs strategy would ipso facto lead to changes in patterns of demand, production and prices and hence in BNI. This problem can be taken care of by periodic revision of BNI as estimated from the core bundle. One would start with the existing set of relative prices, but as and when substantial price changes occur, either because of changes in demand and supply for particular goods and services or through introduction of taxes and subsidies, the BNI needed to meet basic needs would be revised accordingly.

The third issue concerns the existing pattern of tastes and preferences which may not be socially optimal. There are several reasons for this. There is a growing literature which has sought to show how high-powered advertising combined with other sophisticated marketing techniques by large firms, usually foreign-owned and controlled, has succeeded in changing patterns of tastes and often in eliminating indigenous products and industry.[25] There is a large and convincing literature on appropriate products and technologies which has sought to indicate the inappropriateness in the conditions of developing countries of many of the products and technologies imported from industrialised countries.[26] What is not so often emphasized is that many of the indigeneous products whose consumption is sanctified by centuries of social customs and traditions may also constitute serious barriers to a strategy designed to meet the basic material needs of the poor masses. A case in point may be certain types of traditional dwellings which while appropriate in an earlier era may have outlived their usefulness in the modern conditions. Likewise certain types of clothing - sarees may serve as an example (perhaps a bad one) - while gracious and elegant, may interfere seriously with work in modern conditions and may in certain cases represent "excess" consumption. This point can be generalised to other social customs and institutions. A necessary part of purposeful social policy has, therefore, to be to alter patterns of taste and preferences through appropriate leadership,

---

[25] The case of manufactured baby foods to replace mothers' milk has been too much in the news to need more than a gentle reminder.

[26] e.g. Frances Stewart, "Technology and Employment in LDC's" in Edgar O. Edwards, Employment in Developing Countries (Columbia University Press, 1974).

persuasion, education and incentives.[27] Any such changes must necessarily take place gradually over long periods of time except of course in revolutionary situations. But the great potential importance of such action should not be underestimated. Social action of this sort - some political scientists use perhaps somewhat unfortunate terminology "social engineering" to describe this phenomenon - can have profound effects in defining the scope, components, indicators and targets for basic needs, and hence in design and implementation of the strategy.

So far we have dealt with a number of problems surrounding the use of BNI to satisfy private consumption needs. It is necessary now to say a few words about the targets for goods and services provided for and by the community. The ultimate objective must be that through an appropriate combination of BNI and community provided goods and services, the basic needs of all persons and households are met at the stipulated level. How much of this should be achieved through a BNI or collective provision of goods and services - either free or on a subsidised basis - will naturally vary from country to country. In socialist economies, the relative importance of BNI is likely to be less in comparison with societies which place greater reliance on private enterprise. Hence, other things being equal, the stipulated levels of BNI in the former will be lower than in the latter. The above issue should not be confused with ownership of means of production. Certainly

---

[27] No doubt many readers will see in the preceding remarks spectres of authoritarian, dictatorial, or more mildly paternalistic regimes forcing down the throats of the unwilling population their own versions of what is good for the people. This can and indeed does happen. But there are many ways - through discussion, persuasion, peoples' own participation - of altering taste patterns in socially optimal directions. And to suppose that in the absence of such purposeful social action people really have a completely free choice is utterly naive as shown above. It is more likely that the force of the market and official propaganda simply reinforces the trends towards patterns of preference and tastes which may constitute serious obstacles to attaining basic needs targets.

it is conceivable that in a given economy all means of production are in public hands yet the output of goods and services is sold in the market at prices fixed by the state. The BNI in this case must be of a level to permit absorption of a stipulated basket of basic needs. Likewise one can envisage situations where in a largely private enterprise economy, an impressive range of basic goods and services are provided directly by the state either freely or on a subsidised basis, thereby reducing the required level of BNI.

It would be a useful inquiry to pursue whether in the context of a basic needs strategy, one can develop any guidelines as to the appropriate division of responsibility between the community (not necessarily state) and private sectors in production and/or distribution of the basic needs bundle. Many variations are possible. For certain services such as housing and water supply, the community may assume responsibility for laying on the infrastructure and leaving to private or local collective, self-help action to complete the dwellings and provide the taps etc. The crucial role of taxes and subsidies has already been mentioned. They can be used both for altering patterns of consumption and production as well as serve as a deliberate instrument to ensure stipulated absorption of consumption bundle for the poor with a given BNI. Furthermore, state action opens up the possibility of ensuring adequate consumption by particularly disadvantaged groups such as households headed by women, old persons without support from relatives, handicapped persons, abandoned children and unemployables. This action may take the form of straight cash grants or free supply of essential goods and services.

A few concluding remarks may be made on the consumption of public goods and services. First, in most countries, the satisfaction of basic needs is likely to be more speedily attained with the increasing assumption by the public sector of the responsibility for direct provision of certain essential goods and services. This of course implies a substantial redistribution of income through fiscal or other means. Secondly, there is little likelihood of ensuring provision of such goods and services on a mass basis without fundamental changes in their content and delivery systems. This is a particular case of a more general point made above concerning the need for purposeful social action to alter tastes, preferences and customs. Thirdly, their provision must ensure not only availability but also access and usage. This may imply creation of institutions to ensure that benefits from such goods and services reach those most in need.

The final point concerns the inter-related issues of the _level_ at which targets should be set, and the _timing_ and _sequencing_ of their implementation. On target levels, a few observations are in order. In the first place, these should not be set at bare subsistence levels. They should bear some relation to what the society and the world at large regard as "a decent standard of living." This is perhaps an important difference between the basic needs and the poverty line approaches. Secondly, the target-setting cannot be a once-and-for-all exercise. The level of targets must be periodically revised to take account of the evolution of the economy and progress in implementation. Furthermore, as initial targets are attained, they must be revised upwards and improved qualitatively in line with the aspirations of the society. Thirdly, the precise level at which targets are established must reflect social consensus on the degree of economic equality a particular society desires. Other things being given, a society attaching high priority to egalitarian goals will be able to aim at higher target levels for the poorest groups than another which places lower value on this objective. Fourthly, resource availability is an obvious determinant of the level at which targets can be set. A country which is able to mobilise a larger proportion of its income for accumulation through consumption restraints on the better-off groups within the society, or is successful in attracting larger external resources, can, other things being equal, aim at higher targets or achieve given targets more speedily. Fifthly, targets will naturally vary from country to country in accordance with its stage of development. Other things being equal, countries like Bangladesh, Nepal, Chad or Haiti cannot realistically aim to provide the same level and range of basic goods and services for their poverty groups as the more affluent of the developing countries such as Iran, Kuwait, Argentina or Mexico.

In addition to these general remarks, can one say anything more specific by way of guidelines for setting target levels? There are several possibilities here which deserve further investigation. One approach is to use existing consumption levels for a particular group within the society e.g. a national average or some other figure. Another possibility is that the process of the establishment of indicators themselves may suggest targets. Indicators for food requirements are a point in case. Some have argued that the concept of "reference man" duly refined and adapted can yield both indicators and targets.[28] Inter-country comparisons of countries at similar stages of development might yield valuable suggestions for target-setting either for some or all components of basic needs. One can go beyond and look at the "best practice" in particular areas of basic needs in any part of the world and seek to distil guidelines in setting targets.

The question of timing is obviously related to the levels at which targets might be established. Other

---

[28] M. Hopkins, op.cit.

things being equal, the longer the time frame, the more ambitious can the targets be. What is a reasonable planning horizon to aim at? It has been suggested that a ten to fifteen year period would appear to be optimal since it is not too distant to fail "to inspire the present generation and to impart a sense of realism to the programme", nor "too short to cope with the major indicators of destitution."[29]

Then there is the question of priority and sequence in meeting basic needs. Several observations are in order here. The concept of core needs implicitly assigns priority to certain goods and services. However, it was argued above that the specification of core needs does not imply that at the level of a household the entire income be spent only on core needs to the exclusion of all non-essential commodities. Likewise, among the core bundle of goods and services, does it make sense to talk of priorities and sequences? Poor people everywhere obviously consume some quantities of certain essential goods and services. In the case of a commodity like food, survival itself may be at stake without the consumption of certain minimum quantities. But the point is that the consumption of such goods and services is considered wholly inadequate by the society. Thus additional incomes are required to enable increased consumption of essential goods and services. In a typical case, increased income would be used to increase marginal consumption of most essential goods and services as well as of non-essential ones. Is there then no sense in talking about priorities in meeting basic needs? This would be too sweeping a conclusion to draw. Particularly when it comes to the question of publicly provided goods and services, all targets - even for core needs - cannot be reached simultaneously. Thus

---

[29]Khan, op.cit.

choices have to be made and resources allocated accordingly. What criteria might be used in making these choices is an extremely complex question and needs much further thought and analysis. All one can do here is to mention some of the relevant factors. These include community preferences expressed in one way or another, the externalities generated by the consumption of various goods and services, the linkages among different goods and services, the extent of shortfalls between current consumption and desired levels, resource costs, etc.

VII. Role for International Agencies

In the light of the argument that people themselves directly or through their involvement in the national planning systems should determine the scope and content of basic needs, it may legitimately be asked whether international organisations have any role to play in this field. The answer is a clear yes, at any rate in the interim period. One can think of at least four areas in which international organisations can make a distinctive contribution to the development of a basic needs approach:

(i) Given the novelty of basic needs approach, there is a certain minimum amount of conceptual work that may be useful to countries formulating their own approaches. At the methodological level, with which this paper is concerned, this can contribute to a clarification of such issues as scope and content of basic needs, illustrative indicators, measurement and target setting. Of greater, longer term importance is the work associated with the design, formulation and implementation of a basic needs strategy. While some countries have or will evolve their own approaches, there will certainly be a considerable number which may wish to seek the assistance of international organisations in this field. For ILO,

this may particularly be the case in relation to
requests received for the implementation of paragraph
32 of the Declaration of Principles and Programme
of Action adopted at the World Employment
Conference.[30]

(ii) If international agencies are to effectively
contribute to implementation of basic needs strategies
at the national level, as a minimum it is essential
that they come up with an agreed, common approach.
This should ultimately be incorporated in the United
Nations Development Decade Strategy. At a more
practical level, this approach should guide and run
through the operational, research and other
activities of the UN family of organisations. It
could also provide a focus for determining and
channelling development assistance by multilateral
and bilateral agencies.

(iii) An agreed approach at the international level can
facilitate the emergence of some sort of division
of labour among the UN agencies in order to ensure
a certain amount of coherence and consistency in
the effort of the international community.

(iv) An exchange of experience on a comparative basis of
the diverse approaches to formulation and implementation
of basic needs strategies in different countries
can perhaps most efficiently be carried out
through international agencies.

---

[30] See Declaration of Principles and Programme of Action
adopted by the World Employment Conference (WEC/CW/E.I, Geneva,
June, 1976).

CHAPTER III

Some Normative Aspects of a Basic Needs Strategy
by
E. L. H. Lee

To date, normative issues have either received only cursory mention or have been completely assumed away in discussions of Basic Needs strategies. Moreover, these issues, when mentioned, have usually been posed in the form of statements about 'non-material' basic needs, on the same basis as material basic needs. We shall argue that this treatment is unsatisfactory and try to state what we consider are to be the main normative questions that are raised by a Basic Needs Strategy.

There are at least three reasons why discussions of policies for satisfying the basic material needs of a society have, inevitably, to involve a discussion of 'non-material needs' as well. First, there is the obvious point that economics is ultimately about welfare and that welfare involves more than simply a bundle of goods and services. Secondly, deciding on what ought to constitute 'basic' needs and how these are to be satisfied involves value-judgements and raises issues of economic justice and rights. Thirdly, the satisfaction of material needs will involve issues of organisation and of institutional arrangements for the satisfaction of these needs. Alternative institutional arrangements can vary in terms of efficiency as well as in qualitative aspects like 'the degree of participation' or 'quality of work'. It should be noted that all three reasons are inter-related; for example, the degree of economic justice and the type of institutional arrangement are elements in total welfare while institutional arrangements are not independent of conceptions of economic justice.

The first point has been taken care of in the main statement to date on the Basic Needs Strategy.[1] There, a list of proposed basic material needs is supplemented by references to non-material needs like human rights and participation.

A case could be made against the treatment of 'non-material' needs on the same footing as material needs. If some statements about 'human rights' or 'participation' are tagged on to a list of material basic needs such as food and shelter, it could carry several undesirable implications. Ethical absolutes like 'freedom' are treated in the same way as a commodity, thereby giving the impression that it is something to be dispensed at the discretion of a government. Furthermore, this 'commodity analogy' implies a separability between material and non-material needs which is false. The satisfaction of material basic needs is not an end in itself and, therefore, not separable from _how_ these needs are satisfied. It would thus be wrong to pose the problem as though it were one of providing people with a list of material goods, with 'non-material' goods as an optional extra.

Thus although the need for a caveat was recognised, the organic links between the 'non-material' and the material basic needs were not emphasised and crucial normative issues were neglected.[2]

---

[1] ILO "Employment, Growth and Basic Needs" (Geneva, 1976).

[2] It could be argued that none of the previous strategies of development did any such thing, so why should it be demanded of the Basic Needs Strategy? The answer is that it would be prudent for the innovator to explore thoroughly all the implications of the new ideas he is setting forth. This is particularly important for an idea like 'Basic Needs' which at the level of a general exhortation, most people would uncritically accept as a 'good thing'.

I. <u>How and Why do we Specify Basic Needs?</u>

Essentially, the Basic Needs Strategy concentrates on defining an end-state of material consumption which it is the purpose of 'development' to attain. The rationale is the persistance of absolute poverty, manifested by mass destitution, in spite of a quarter of a century of 'development' effort and the consequent need to raise the destitute, as a matter of priority, to a level where all their basic needs are satisfied. This basic thrust is clear and unexceptional as it stands but many questions are left unanswered.

For instance, one might ask whether this consumption end-state is to be understood as a 'subjective minimum of satisfaction ...or...as an objective minimum of conditions'?[3] If, as seems to be clearly implied, it is the latter then the question arises as to the content of this objective minimum and by what means its observance is to be enforced. Pigou, for instance, in discussing a similar problem maintained that "the conditions must be conditions, not in respect of one aspect of life only, but in general. Thus the minimum includes some defined quantity and quality of house accommodation, of medical care, of education, of food, of leisure, of the apparatus of sanitary convenience and safety where work is carried on and so on".[4] He argued that observance must be absolute and simultaneous. "A man must not be permitted to fall below the minimum in one department in order that he may rise above it in others...The State must not permit anywhere hours of child labour or of women's labour or conditions of housing accommodation incompatible with the minimum standard, on the ground that, by resort to them, some given family could, and, without resort to them, it could not support itself; for, if that is the fact, the family ought not to be required to support itself".[5] Pigou's conclusions are clearly traceable to his utilitarian assumptions; what are the conclusions of the Basic Needs Strategy and to what are they traceable? Clearly this is

---

[3] A. C. Pigou "The Economics of Welfare", (MacMillan, London 1962) p.759.

[4] Ibid, p.759.

[5] Ibid, p.760

not a trivial objection. If one busies oneself with problems such as whether there should be a 'core' or a more extensive list of basic needs, and with estimating 'shortfalls' of basic needs, then it is incumbent upon one to say _how_ the absorption of these items are to be ensured. Such exercises are clearly prescriptive (i.e. that such and such a bundle of goods and services _ought_ to be consumed) yet they are curiously silent on how this might be achieved.

The methodology developed thus far oscillates between two contradictory principles for determining the level and composition of basic needs. The first might be termed a 'technocratic approach' where needs are deduced from biological and other scientific data. For instance, the requirements for food are deduced from the nutritional needs of the human organism and are expressed in terms of calories and proteins, or the need for housing and clothing from the degree of protection required against the physical environment. The analytical tool here is the concept of a 'reference man'. The opposite principle is that of democratic choice, that 'the people' should specify their needs through some process of collective decision making. Note that the two principles may conflict; the 'technological' principle will yield a bundle of 'characteristics' like calories or cubic metres of space[6] which are not commodities and hence not the categories in terms of which the democratic collective choice will be expressed. If the technological principle is taken to its logical extension, the analysis would become one of finding a least-cost solution for satisfying the vector of basic needs 'characteristics'. In this case, sets of basic needs goods derived from the two principles are unlikely to overlap and hence would conflict. Thus it is invalid to work with both principles

---

[6] See K. J. Lancaster "A New Approach to Consumer Theory" _Journal of Political Economy_ Vol.74 (1966) for a discussion of the difference between 'characteristics' and commodities.

simultaneously and, especially, to work with the technocratic principle in isolation of how absorption is to be ensured.

One could muddy the water further by considering a third principle, that of revealed preference. The procedure here would be to define exogenously a combination of basic needs goods and to deduce from consumption data the level of income which would ensure that these goods are actually purchased and consumed. The assumption is that individual tastes, as revealed by the market behaviour of the marginal unit which just consumes the entire basic needs bundle, would ensure absorption. This approach has great intuitive appeal yet its distinctness should not be overlooked. It is similar to the technological approach in so far as the basic needs bundle must be exogenously determined, though not necessarily on the same basis. Unlike that approach, however, it is mindful of tastes[7] and deals in terms of actual marketed commodities and not in terms of 'characteristics'. It is clear at the same time that the two approaches are not necessarily incompatible and indeed could be judiciously combined. They both differ, however, from the principle of collective choice which, in essence, is contractuarian in the Rawlsian sense.[8] People agree on a list of basic commodities which their collective effort should produce. The choice could also extend to questions of the necessary productive and distributive arrangements for attaining these objectives. Furthermore, in this conception there is no role for the manipulation of tastes or consumption patterns; the choice is essentially voluntary with no preconceived outcomes to impose and hence there would be no need to manipulate consumption behaviour to fit this preconceived pattern.

---

[7] Note, however, that this approach, in inferring preferences from observed market behaviour implicitly assumes that the prevailing income-distribution and the existing tastes are 'correct'. See Chapter II and IV of this volume for a fuller discussion of these issues.

[8] See J. Rawls "Distributive Justice" in E. S. Phelps (ed.) Economic Justice (London, 1973). We think here of "an agreement among free and independent persons in an original position of equality..."(p.321).

It should be clear, therefore, that the specification of basic needs cannot be done in isolation from normative considerations. Similarly, we must also bring these normative considerations to bear when we answer the inevitable question of why a list of basic needs is being specified. To proceed to somehow quantify basic needs without careful prior attention to these two questions and to believe that the resulting quantification will contribute substantially to 'solving' world poverty is, to say the least, quixotic.

II. Basic Rights and Basic Needs

It is important not to confuse basic needs with basic rights. 'Basic human rights' has, for instance, been included as an item in a list of basic needs.[9] It is obscure, however, how one can 'need' a 'right'; a right has an autonomous existence, quite independent of whether one has a need for it or not, by virtue of some theory of law. A 'need' for a right cannot create a right, neither can a right be denied because it is in some sense not needed.

There is some danger that in speaking of 'priority being given to basic needs' and the 'dethronement of GDP', one may lose sight of the fact that the satisfaction of basic needs is not an end in itself. For example, it cannot be a justification for the violation of basic human rights.[10] Human rights are inviolable and the setting of basic needs targets does not imply that meeting these targets are desirable at any cost. For example, a development strategy based on political repression could perhaps succeed in meeting basic needs in a narrow quantitative sense[11]

---

[9] P. Streeten "Basic Needs: An issues paper " (mimeo., IBRD, Washington 1977) p.6.

[10] We could formulate it in terms of the Kantian principle that people are ends and not merely means; they may not be sacrificed or used for the achieving of other ends without their consent.

[11] "Prisoners in rich countries often have access to more things and services than members of their families, but they have no say in how things are to be made and cannot decide what to do with them...they are degraded to the status of mere consumers" (I. Illich 'Tools for Conviviality [Fontana, London 1975] p.24). Note that while we concede that material needs can be met in this narrow sense, we by no means imply that the violation of rights was a necessary condition for the provision of those material needs.

but this would clearly be an unacceptable option. Equally unacceptable would be a system which 'satisfies' material needs without any regard to the conditions of work or the cost in terms of physical effort.

Basic needs also impinge upon the question of rights in the context of economic justice. Firstly, even when viewed as a static end-state, a prescription for satisfying basic needs raises issues concerning principles of rewards and deserts. Does the acceptance of 'basic needs' for instance, imply the acceptance of need as a criterion for wage payment? How might the needs of the unemployed, aged or unemployable be met? Thus, although it is clearly implied that a basic needs strategy is based on the satisfaction of basic needs via a change in the structure of production, as opposed to consumption transfers (or welfare schemes), the question of meeting the needs of those outside the production process has still to be faced.

The question of rights surfaces with even greater force when the satisfaction of basic needs is considered as implying some generating process. A central part of this process would be redistributive and requiring substantial state intervention and hence it would be necessary to specify the underlying justification. Is it based on the exploitative nature of present economic institutions, on the acceptance of the Rawlsian difference principle or on some other principle? The question is not irrelevant because, in the absence of any such statement, one is open to the charge of being oblivious to important questions about rights and economic justice.[12]

---

[12] See for instance D. Lall "Distribution and Development: A review article" World Development Vol.4, No.9, pp.725-738, who questions redistributive strategies using arguments derived from R. A. Nozick "Anarchy, State and Utopia". (Blackwell, Oxford 1974)

III. Basic Needs and Equality

Meeting basic needs in poor societies hinges crucially upon the degree of equality that can be made to prevail. This is true in several senses. First, the degree of equality can be considered as an element in the social welfare function, an attribute desirable in its own right. This probably assumes a sharper significance in a poor society, where destitution is juxtaposed with affluence, than in a richer one. Moreover, equality of sacrifice would be an important consideration in motivating and mobilising people.

Secondly, a maximum permissible degree of inequality might have to be imposed in poor societies for the simple reason that average income is so low that a wide dispersion around this average would leave large numbers in destitution.[13] Furthermore, levels of basic needs should not be set too far below the average since this would loosen the constraint on governments to redistribute significantly. If this were not done, it would be possible to set basic needs at such a low level that the concept degenerates into a modern variant of Poor Laws, with each country providing soup kitchens 'appropriate to their level of development'. The same objection would apply to any attempt to interpret a basic needs policy in terms of how consumption could be pared down subject to the constraint of satisfying a vector of basic needs 'characteristics' derived from the 'technological' approach referred to earlier.

---

[13] In principle, it is possible to conceive of situations where total income is so low that even a completely equal distribution would be below 'basic needs'. In this case we can no longer speak of basic needs being exclusively a 'national' problem, if there is some universal principle about meeting needs being upheld. It is doubtful, however, if one can realistically think of a society that would be chronically unable to meet the basic needs which it has defined for itself, given a high degree of equality.

Thirdly, a broad degree of equality in political and economic power is a pre-condition for satisfying basic needs efficiently. 'Participation', for instance, cannot be meaningful unless it is based on equality in the political and economic base. At the same time 'popular participation' is also a highly efficient way of satisfying many basic needs of the people. This would be especially true for community services such as health and education. Innovative ways of meeting these needs through popular participation are likely to ensure greater efficiency, to provide a product more closely related to the needs of the people and also to satisfy, through the production process itself, the goal of popular involvement. It is essential, therefore, that the discussion of basic needs targets in this field should not give the impression that existing systems are the only viable ones and that meeting basic needs necessarily requires 'more of the same'.

Ensuring greater equality through the removal of social institutions that discriminate against minorities or hinder equal access in social and economic life, is a pre-condition for mobilising the energies of the people towards satisfying their basic needs. Greater equality, in this broad sense, is thus an inherent part of a Basic Needs Strategy.

IV. The Political Economy of Basic Needs Satisfaction

In the previous section some reasons were advanced to explain why equality was both intrinsically desirable as well as being a necessary condition for meeting basic needs. In this section we shall elaborate on the latter point by showing that implementing a basic needs strategy inevitably demands a large measure of structural change and redistribution. This is a normative consideration which ought to be made explicit.

The claim of novelty for a basic needs strategy rests on a rejection of previous development strategies because of their observed failure to alleviate mass poverty. The implicit belief is that 'false doctrines' explain past failures and that a new 'strategy' will be instrumental in bringing about change. Even without resorting to extreme scepticism about the independent force of ideas, one can identify several reasons for pessimism.

A basic point is the obvious one about the nature of the state and the interests it represents. Suffice it to say that one cannot blithely assume a harmony of interests and that the problem of satisfying basic needs cannot be abstracted into a programming exercise involving needs and resource availabilities. We shall illustrate by enumerating several inherent contradictions.

A fundamental implication of adopting a basic needs strategy is the need for a shift in the composition of output in favour of necessities.[14] In most developing countries the composition of output has been shaped by a highly skewed pattern of income distribution and could be described as 'oligarchic'. A large proportion of total resources is devoted to the luxury consumption of a few. There would clearly be political problems in bringing about a renunciation of such consumption, not only because it is the 'raison d'être' for the élite, but also because they might be functional to the prevailing socio-economic system.[15] Other obstacles would include the vested interests of producers and importers of these commodities and the fact that the tastes of those on the margins of poverty might have been so shaped by the existing pattern of production (and advertising) that they aspire and hence acquiesce to such a pattern of consumption.[16]

---

[14] We concentrate on the composition of output because it is the key concept in the basic needs strategy; poverty is manifested by the <u>absence</u> of basic goods and services for the poor and the solution is to <u>supply</u> these items. We are aware, of course, of the <u>interdependence</u> between the composition of output, the distribution of income and the pattern of ownership of productive assets.

[15] e.g. as part of a 'con-mech' system. See C. Elliot "Patterns of Poverty in the Third World" (Praeger, New York, 1975). The obverse point about poverty being functional to a process of accumulation would also be equally valid.

[16] This is an aspect of a more general point that an unequal distribution of income combined with a simple majority rule of decision making will result in the concentration of the benefits of any redistributive measures on those in the middle range of incomes (see R. A. Nozick op. cit., pp.274-275 for an ingenious exposition). The relevance for basic needs is that market developing economies are characterised by both great inequality and a claim to being democratic.

The same resistance to a change in the composition of output could arise with some socially provided services such as medical services, education and public utilities. Sophisticated medical services, 'good' higher education and motorways are obviously important items in élite 'needs', yet at the same time they preempt resources for mass medical services, basic education and public transport respectively. In addition, there would be the vested interests of the professions; "Basic needs are defined as those that international professions can meet. Since the local production of these wares is to the advantage of highly schooled national élites, a county's doctors and teachers and engineers will defend it as an antidote to foreign domination. The knowledge-capitalism of professional imperialism subjugates people more imperceptibly than and as effectively as international finance or weaponry."[17]

Inequality not only shapes <u>what</u> is produced but also determines entitlement to those basic goods and services that <u>are</u> available. Food is a case in point. An unequal distribution of purchasing power determines that scarce land is used to produce "a tridde of milk and meat instead of millet and soya beans".[18] This constrains the choices available to the poor. In addition, however, purchasing power could also exclude the poor from the consumption of those basic food items that are available especially during famines and other abnormal circumstances.[19] Thus, even if the prevailing distribution of purchasing power permits the satisfaction of basic food needs during normal periods it provides no <u>guarantee</u> of a permanent satisfaction of these needs. This would suggest that inequality within a market economy not only militates against the production of basic goods but it also menaces

---

[17] I. Illich op. cit.

[18] M. Lipton <u>"Why poor people stay poor"</u> (Temple Smith, London, 1977).

[19] K. B. Griffin "The Fundamental Causes of World Hunger", (mimeo. Queen Elisabeth House, Oxford).

the continued satisfaction of needs even after basic need targets are 'met'. Thus even if the composition of output could be altered, mechanisms would still have to be found to ensure that need is both a necessary and sufficient condition for continued access to basic goods.

The contradictions do not exist only with regard to what is available and who consumes how much. Since the ownership of assets determines the distribution of incomes and through it creates the conflict of interest in demand, we cannot discuss a change in the composition of output in isolation from a change in the ownership of productive assets. For example, it would be inconsistent to ask capitalists to switch to the production of necessities and yet not worry about the impact of profits on the pattern of demand.

CHAPTER IV

Basic Need Targets:
An Illustrative Exercise in Identification and Quantification
With Reference to Bangladesh *
by
A.R. Khan

To plan for the satisfaction of an absolute level of basic needs of a society it is necessary to begin with the resolution of the following two issues:

(a) the identification of the scope of basic needs, i.e., the preparation of a list of items of private and social consumption which are considered to be essential for decent human existence; and

(b) the quantification of the target per capita level of consumption of each of these items above which all individuals and households must be raised within a stipulated time period.

I. The Scope of Basic Needs

Apparently it is impossible to have agreement between any two thinking human beings about which items of consumption are basic to decent human existence and hence should be included in a basic needs basket. There are no objective criteria to define the contents of a minimum consumption bundle. One possible solution would appear to be the construction of a list of items in order of priority - to have a hierarchically ordered set of basic needs. The underlying idea is that the planners in a society should try to satisfy as many of them as possible in order of priority. However, it is not easy to establish such an ordering. The only meaningful way to settle the issue would be to ask the members of the society what their priorities are. As we hope to show later, consumers cannot realistically be thought of as ordering goods and services as such. They consume various items simultaneously, i.e., they make comparisons between _incremental_ changes in the volume of goods and do not compare, for example, the _full_ satisfaction of

---

* The paper was originally presented at the Bangladesh National Workshop on Employment Policy, Dacca, January 1977.

nutritional requirements with the _full_ satisfaction of shelter. The question is how much of each is possible. Without bringing quantities into explicit consideration it is meaningless to try to determine how the consumers order various items in terms of importance.

Even when quantities are made explicit the ordering of the different members would be different. The planner would then be faced with the virtually impossible task of weighting individual preferences. The problem would be rendered even more difficult by the consideration that individual ordering would be an inappropriate indicator in the presence of consumption externalities.

While the above qualification should not be discarded as facetious we must recognise that in reality a practical planner often finds it possible to define _a core_ of basic needs that seems surprisingly robust. This is particularly the case in a situation of extreme poverty and deprivation as is found in countries like Bangladesh.

II. Some Indicators of Shortfall from Basic Needs in Bangladesh

During 1962-64, the period covered by the most recent Nutrition Survey for which results are available, 45.7 per cent of the rural population and 76.4 per cent of the urban population in Bangladesh had a daily intake of calories below the minimum required level. The gap between the required level and the actual intake was greater for protein, respectively 60.8 and 77.2 per cent for rural and urban population. Virtually the entire population suffered from an inadequate intake of one or the other kind of vitamin.[1]

Although the results of the recently completed Nutrition Survey are not yet available it seems beyond doubt that the situation today is much worse. By 1975 the average real income was lower and the distribution of real income was worse as

---

[1] These data are based on the U.S. Department of Health, Education and Welfare, _Nutrition Survey of East Pakistan, March 1962 - January 1964_, May 1966.

compared to the early and mid 1960s.² Since the autumn of 1975 the per capita intake of food has improved though it is still substantially below the level that prevailed in the early and mid 1960s. It is reasonable to suppose that today well over half the population suffer from inadequate intake of calories and that the protein and vitamin gaps are correspondingly greater.

Per capita consumption of clothing in rural Bangladesh in 1963-64 averaged 8.8 square yards of coarse cloth equivalent. Those who had a per capita consumption of less than 7.3 square yards constituted more than 40 per cent of the rural population. The need for clothing arises out of factors such as environmental protection and, especially for women in a traditional society, the social standards of decency. For a Bengali woman a *sari* is the minimum acceptable covering deemed necessary for public appearance. Only for the poorest does this constitute the sole item of dress and the minimum size is over 6 square yards. Assume that an average family of 6 persons at the 40th percentile (in terms of population) in the income scale has 2 male, 2 female and 2 child members. Assume further that the clothing requirements of an adult male and a child are respectively 1/2 and 1/4 of that of an adult female. The data on the distribution of consumption of cloth indicate that even under these assumptions an adult female of such a family will have just about two coarse and short saris per year as her only clothing.³ This may be barely enough to protect her from socially unacceptable standards of clothing.

However, let us look at the distribution of clothing more closely. The above consumption levels include the entire consumption of cloth - from bed cloth to the shroud - not only the clothing. Secondly, the above circumstances applied to

---

² See A.R. Khan, *Poverty and Inequality in Rural Bangladesh*, (ILO, World Employment Programme Working Paper, 1976.)

³ Such a family will have 3.5 adult female equivalent of consumers of cloth and a total of 43.8 square yards (= 7.3 x 6) of cloth per year. Thus the availability per adult female equivalent will be 12.5 yards.

the average family at the 40th percentile from below in the income distribution scale. Those in the bottom 2 or 3 deciles had much lower levels of consumption of clothing. It is perhaps reasonable to suppose that the bottom fifth or the bottom quarter of the rural population had such a low level of clothing per capita in the 1960s as to be unable to guarantee their women freedom from an acute sense of social shame.[4] Today the situation is a good deal worse. The average consumption of cloth fell to less than 5 yards per person by 1973 and remains today below the level that prevailed in the 1960s.[5]

On housing little information is available for the rural areas. According to the 1961 Census only 2 per cent of the rural dwelling units were permanent structures. Over 77 per cent were "temporary structures" while the rest were not classified. According to the available family expenditure surveys a very high proportion of expenditure on housing consists of repair and maintenance. A hut that has to be replaced completely every 2 or 3 years can hardly be called building capital. They seldom provide protection from the monsoon rain or from the rather mild winter. For urban housing we have a little better information based on a survey of 1,100 dwellings in the three largest urban industrial centres during the 1960s.[6] The house of an average family had 3.7 persons per room. Seventy one per cent of these houses were temporary constructions without any masonry, 56 per cent had only one room, 82 per cent had no water connection and 97 per cent were without electricity. Today, the housing conditions are almost certainly worse.

---

[4] The information on the distribution of consumption of cloth in the rural areas is based on the Quarterly Survey of Current Economic Conditions (QSCEC) for 1963-64 carried out by the Pakistan C.S.O. In the urban areas per capita consumption of cloth was higher. But, since 93 per cent of the people lived in the rural areas during the mid 1960s the national consumption and its distribution was about the same as that of the rural areas.

[5] Planning Commission, Government of Bangladesh, The First Five-Year Plan, p. 21.

[6] C.S.O. (Pakistan), Statistical Yearbook 1968.

III. The Identification of a Core of Basic Needs for Bangladesh

In a situation as depicted above will a planner be too widely off the mark if he were to identify food, clothing and shelter as the core of a basic needs programme? The very first question we should face is whether the satisfaction of such a core will provide a balanced bundle of consumption goods. Although these three items account for an overwhelming proportion of the budget of an average consumer in Bangladesh, it is by no means true that all other needs can be neglected. What will happen to the consumption level of these other goods and services?

At this stage we must involve ourselves in the question of the mechanism of satisfying basic needs. Even in a highly planned society (e.g., China) the actual absorption of food, clothing and most other consumption goods depends by and large on the decision of the individual consuming units like households. It is unthinkable to mount a consumption programme independent of such consumer preferences. It is certainly true that the society can powerfully influence the outcome by such means as altering the relative prices, providing some items of consumption socially and, over a longer period, influencing private preferences. But once these measures of social intervention are introduced the actual absorption of the various items remains a matter of individual and household preferences.

It, therefore, does not make sense to set up independent basic needs targets for various items that are inconsistent in the context of what adjustments in consumer preferences can be achieved by meaningful and efficient social intervention. Given such intervention the instrument for the implementation of a basic needs programme will be the distribution of income. If the planner wants a household to have food consumption equivalent to 2,500 calories of energy per capita then he must identify the level of income that, given the role of social intervention reflected in relative prices etc., would induce the household to spend an adequate amount on food. Such household decisions would in the process ensure that the requirement

of other items of consumption that the household values as
much as the marginal units of the core items are satisfied.
In this sense the identification of a core of basic needs
such as the one illustrated above for Bangladesh may be
quite adequate. Indeed there would even seem to be a case
for identifying a single basic item. We shall return to this
theme when we discuss the problem of quantifying basic needs.

The next points to consider are those of adequacy and
feasibility. The criterion of adequacy is needed to establish
that the proposed core is a sufficiently ambitious programme
which, if successfully implemented, would significantly alter
the quality of life for the vast number of population. The
criterion of feasibility is the other side of the coin. It
is needed to find out if the satisfaction of the core items
would require an amount of resources which are within the
capacity of the society to generate.

None of these criteria can be applied without some
notion of a time horizon. So, let us begin by trying to
define a reasonable planning horizon. The two suggestions
that emerge from the historical practices are:

(a) a five-year period over which the quinquennial
development plans are formulated; and

(b) a twenty or twenty-five year period over which
perspective plans used to be outlined during the
Pakistan days.

In our view both these time periods are inappropriate for
a basic needs plan. A five-year period is too short to cope
with the major indicators of destitution. A twenty or twenty-
five year horizon, in a society in which the expectation of
life at birth is only 45 odd years, is too distant to inspire
the present generation and to impart a sense of realism for
the programme. Something like ten to fifteen years, two or
three successive five-year plans, seems to be a reasonable
time period over which to plan substantial improvements. Such
a horizon would not be too distant in terms of popular aspira-
tion.

Over a ten to fifteen year period, i.e., approximately
over the period to be covered by the Second, Third and possibly

the Fourth Five-year Plans, the objective of

(a) raising more than half the population, who are currently starved of calories, above the minimum required level;

(b) providing socially acceptable minimum amount of clothing to about a quarter or so of the people who are currently unable to protect themselves from intense social shame due to inadequate clothing; and

(c) providing minimum shelter in the form of basic housing would appear to be quite an ambitious target.

It should be reiterated that the development effort that would be required to achieve this target will not merely consist of producing and/or supplying the additional food, clothing and housing to bring the currently deprived households above the acceptable level. It will be necessary to produce and/or supply the whole range of goods that will be demanded by these households when their incomes are raised above the minimum level consistent with the adequate absorption of these basic needs items. Moreover, given the social realities, it will be impossible to limit income increases to only those who are currently deprived; many of those who are above the poverty line today will have to be conceded income increases though, hopefully, not in the proportion for those below the poverty line.[7] Thus the total effort will have to be a very large one. Such a programme will constitute a major challenge to the ability of this poor society to generate resources and implement projects. But it will not be such an impossibly ambitious exercise as to be completely written off as unfeasible.

---

[7] As we hope to show later, the acceptance of the *existing* social reality, e.g., the present distribution of income and the laws and institutions determining the participation of the people, will make it impossible to implement any basic needs programme. On the other hand, one must not disregard the constraints that will continue to exist even after a reasonable transformation of existing reality.

We have already sounded the warning that social intervention will have to be geared to permit the adequate absorption of certain goods and services which provide consumption externalities. To leave the absorption of these items to be decided entirely by the consumers themselves will result in a situation in which the individual's subjective needs will be satisfied while the society's needs will remain unsatisfied. In this category will fall services like health and education. A related problem is with those goods and services for which private production and distribution cannot be depended upon as a means of satisfying basic needs either because of important economies of scale in relation to the current level of effective demand or because it is difficult to make the market work as a distributive mechanism. The supply of drinking water in rural areas is an example. These items must be made explicit in the list of basic needs and appropriate mechanism must be devised for their adequate absorption. Otherwise the principle of satisfying the demand for the core items will result in an inadequate demand for these goods and services.

How should we prepare a list of such items? One criterion is to order items according to the degree of externality and select some from the top. It is widely believed that a health service should head the list and be followed by education. While we find the case for their inclusion a very convincing one we shall argue later that the contents of these services in a basic needs programme for Bangladesh should be very different from the conventional ones. To these we would suggest the addition of two more items:

(a) drinking water which can be provided at relatively low cost and has high externality, and

(b) access to contraception.

The scope of basic needs for Bangladesh is then the collection of the following seven items:

1. Food
2. Clothing
3. Shelter
4. Health
5. Education
6. Drinking Water
7. Contraception

IV. <u>The Sequence of Quantification</u>

To quantify basic needs one should begin by estimating the acceptable levels of the "private consumption" items (e.g., the first three in the above list). The next step is to determine the level of income that would permit the absorption of the stipulated levels of the private consumption goods. Let us name it the basic needs level of personal income (BNI). Note, however, that the achievement of BNI will not satisfy all basic needs. For items 4 – 7 the level of demand generated by BNI will be below the basic needs level. The next step, therefore, consists of estimating the acceptable levels of these remaining items – those which provide large positive externalities.

It may appear inconsistent to estimate BNI from independent estimates of the required levels of three items of basic needs. Indeed, except for a rare coincidence, the indicated BNI would be different in each of the three cases. Should we then look for the "dominant item of basic need" – the one whose adequate absorption automatically ensures that of the rest of the private consumption items? One can think of arguments against this. First, consumption patterns change over time, and in response to factors such as changes in relative prices, so that the "dominant item" may easily change. Thus it is safer to use a core bundle rather than a single item. Secondly, the dominant item method may easily give too high a level of BNI. Suppose in a given situation the BNI dictated by the basic need level of item x is way above that of BNI dictated by the basic need levels of all other goods. In a situation like this it will be easier to satisfy the basic need for item x by changing the relative prices or by public distribution. Indeed, in this case the commodity x should be

in the nature of the externality providing goods. We shall
return to this problem when we discuss the quantification
of basic needs.

One may ask why do we need to define a bundle of basic
needs items? Why is it not enough to identify a basic needs
income (BNI) level and use that in all exercises? The answer
is that a BNI can only be estimated on the basis of a core
of basic needs. There is a clear interpretation of a BNI
that satisfies minimum food requirement and minimum requirement
of clothing and shelter. Unless one is able to quantify these
basic needs there is no objective way of determining BNI.

Secondly, the achievement of BNI will not be enough.
As we have discussed above, the demand for the externality
providing goods and services will not be met by BNI unless of
course we opt for a "market strategy" to satisfy all demands
in which case the stipulated BNI will be absurdly high.

It should be clearly understood that in our system the BNI
is just the instrument to implement the "private consumption"
part of the basic needs programme. We are not suggesting that
the target itself should be set in terms of a BNI, that such
a BNI should be calculated for a benchmark year and be revised
for changes in prices in subsequent years. The concept of
constant real income is not at all precise and it is somewhat
dangerous to work with a real BNI measurement that is divorced
for too long from an explicit enumeration of the bundle of
basic needs that it is intended to satisfy. Such an income
measurement quickly becomes a fetish and the ritual of subsequent adjustment by cost of living indices is carried out
without making sure that the stipulated level still satisfies
the same basic needs.

V. The Quantification of the "Private Consumption" Items in the Basic Needs Bundle

a. Food

A balanced diet that satisfies all kinds of requirements
(e.g., calories, proteins and vitamins) and is reasonably
consistent with consumers' preferences in Bangladesh would be
very expensive in relation to the actual dietary standards.

Let us, therefore, lower our basic need standard for food and set the less ambitious goal of achieving an adequate level of calorie intake.[8] The FAO estimate of the calorie requirement for an average person in Bangladesh (based on height, weight, age, sex and environmental temperature) is about 2,150 per day. But it would clearly be wrong to use this as the per capita calorie target for every family. The requirement is much greater for households engaged in heavy physical labour. Typically such families are located in the lower range of the income scale. To determine the basic need level of calorie intake we must estimate the requirement of the lowest income groups. For this we need a good deal of detailed information. The following exercise is essentially illustrative.

The overwhelming majority of the poorest quarter of the population of Bangladesh consists of rural peasants and labourers. The 1963-64 QSCEC shows that among the poorest quarter of the rural households the ratio of earners to total members was about 0.3. Thus it is reasonable to assume that 30 per cent of the members of such households are engaged in heavy agricultural work. Let us assume that the calorie requirement of the remaining 70 per cent is the same as that for an average person. For the 30 per cent who undertake heavy physical work we must provide additional energy. Once again, we require carefully established measurements of additional calorie requirement for such work. For our purpose, let us assume that the additional calorie required by an agricultural labourer over what is required by an average Bengalee is equivalent to the difference between the calorie requirement for 8 hours' heavy work and 8 hours' light or industrial work. An Indian study puts this differential at 1,300 calories for men and 900 calories for women.[9] Assuming that 2/3 of those who are engaged in heavy work are men the weighted average of additional calorie required per person involved in heavy work turns out to be 1,167. Thus for an average family with 30 per cent

---

[8] At this stage we feel that the collaboration of the dieticians is required to establish the extent of protein and vitamin gap once the calorie gap is closed. Claims have been made by some dieticians that our traditional measurements may be misleading, that by bridging the calorie gap we virtually ensure that other gaps are also eliminated.

[9] P.V. Sukhatme, *Feeding India's Growing Millions*, Asia Publishing House, London 1965.

of its members engaged in heavy manual work the per capita calorie requirement for the family as a whole would be 2,500 per day.[10]

It may be argued that in view of the widespread underemployment the calorie requirement should be lower. Our answer to this is that the implementation of a basic needs programme in a poor country like Bangladesh is impossible without the full use of the labour force - a situation that will not permit significant under-employment.

What about the argument that as the basic needs target this is far too high in view of the fact that many white collar sedentary workers will require far less calories than this? This takes us back to the question of the mechanism of implementing the basic needs programme. In the foreseeable future in Bangladesh the social conditions will not permit a distribution of income that places a sedentary worker below an agricultural labourer even if widespread redistribution takes place. Indeed, there does not seem to exist any society in the contemporary world in which such a distribution is the rule rather than an exception. Since the way to enable an agricultural labourer to have the stipulated calories is to give him an income high enough to induce him to do so and since white collar workers will have to be paid more due to the economic laws that are dictated by the historical evolution of the society to its present circumstances, the latter will have a _possible_ level of consumption in excess of their basic need. They will, of course, not have a correspondingly higher level of food consumption. Instead, they will spend their income on other goods and services.

At this stage it is useful to note that between the estimation of basic needs and the planning of production there are a number of stages through which a planner must go. The estimation of basic needs does not directly provide us with an estimation of final consumption demand; it merely provides us

---

[10] This is worked out as follows: $0.7 (2,150) + 0.3 (2,150 + 1,167) = 2,500$.

with the floor below which the poor must not fall. But the
actual comsumption of individual households will depend on
their preferences and incomes. Thus the estimation of aggregate
consumption demand will require the knowledge of the distribution
of income and of the pattern of demand for various income
groups for the commodity in question. Once aggregate consumption for a target basic need is estimated the level of required
production and/or supply can be determined by taking into
account the interdependence among activities.

Most, but by no means all, households will consume more
than the basic need level of each item. Some items of basic
need (e.g., calories but, more probably, an individual item
like coarse grain that supplies calories) may easily be an
inferior good for relatively higher levels of income.

b. <u>Clothing</u>

Once we move away from food we are on less sure ground.
The basic need level of clothing has to be estimated on criteria
which are more arbitrary than that for food needed for survival.
Still, one can think of some reasonable criteria to define a
minimum acceptable standard of clothing although it is very
difficult to translate such criteria into actual quantities.

The two criteria that I can think of have already been
discussed above. The first is the consideration of environmental protection while the second is the consideration of
socially acceptable standards of decency. I have expressed
the opinion that for women in Bangladesh the second criterion
is the dominant one. If women are clad adequately to fulfil
the minimum social standard of decency then they will also have
reasonable environmental protection. It needs to be established
if the same is true of men and children.

As I have argued above, approximately 12 square yards of
cotton textile per year is the absolute minimum standard below
which a woman would be unable to appear publicly. For an adult
man 6 square yards per year, providing two <u>lungis</u>, may serve
such a standard and for a child 3 yards may serve similar
purpose. All these estimates are merely illustrative and
need to be established after careful investigation.

For an average family of two adult males, two adult females and two children the annual requirement of clothing will thus be 42 yards or 7 yards per capita. Note that this amount will be required only for clothing and that the need for other textile articles (e.g., bed clothes) will have to be satisfied separately. One may want to add something extra for protection from the three months of rather mild winter. I tend to think that a three yard piece of flannel will provide such protection over a number of years.

It is almost certainly inappropriate to estimate the consumption response of an agricultural labourer by looking at the cross section behaviour of the rural population. Those who are currently able to reach a per capita daily calorie intake of 2,500 perhaps do not need or want calories nearly as much as the poorer people. It is likely that an agricultural labourer will consume 2,500 calories at an income level considerably lower than that of the household which currently does so. In other words the income elasticity of demand by the agricultural labourers for calories is higher than the one estimated on the basis of cross section observation of household behaviour. Even so, an income elasticity of 2/3 is probably the upper limit for such consumers in the relevant income range. Using this estimate one finds that to achieve a per capita daily calorie intake of 2,500 a family will require a per capita monthly income of about Taka 34 at 1963-64 prices.[11] Only about 20 per cent of the population were above that income level in 1963-64. But a family at that income level consumed significantly more cloth than the basic need level calculated by us above. Thus, unless the relative prices change wildly, the satisfaction of basic food need will automatically provide a level of clothing consumption that is above the amount that might be the minimum required for environmental protection and social standards of decency.

---

[11] This is on the assumption that the income adjustment takes place in a single period and that over the range of income adjustment the income elasticity is 2/3. If the income adjustment takes place over a number of years and if the income elasticity remains constant over these years then the increase in income will have to be higher because of different rates of compounding for calories and income. This is why the calculations in the next section are a little different.

c. Shelter

To try to estimate the basic need for housing is even more difficult, if only because it is important to specify both qualitative and quantitative standards. Lack of adequate information about the benchmark condition is a further difficulty in the way of proper estimation of feasible and desirable improvement.

Over 90 per cent of the families live in villages where most of the dwelling units are simple constructions of bamboo and straw built by the occupants themselves with some local help. Few of them have basic facilities such as toilet and water supply. Most of them are unable to provide protection from monsoon rain or insulation from winter air. Most of them are vulnerable to storms and cyclones which lash the country from time to time.

In terms of quantity perhaps for an average family of six persons we could specify basic housing need as consisting of two rooms (each about 150 square feet) with a tiny space for cooking. Of far greater importance is the specification of quality. It is totally unrealistic to think of providing permanent brick structures for everyone within the foreseeable future. The structure will continue to be based on the same kind of materials as are in use now, although there is a lot of scope for appropriate and specific technological improvement. The structure should, however, be adapted to provide protection from rain and wind and not give in too easily in the face of moderate cyclones and storms. It should contain or have access to reasonable, though not necessarily modern, toilet facilities.

To achieve the basic housing target the first problem to overcome is the guarantee of access to the piece of land on which the house would stand. In the rural areas this access will have to be provided by suitable legal and institutional changes if a beginning is to be made towards the satisfaction of basic housing need. The next thing that might be provided is some improved ideas about sanitary conditions (e.g., how to set up simple but hygienic toilet facilities) and housing design (how to improve the insulation of the thatched roof). Beyond these measures, which are broadly similar to those of providing the goods and services that embody externalities, the implementation of the programme will have to be left to the individual households and local self help efforts through appropriate inducements of higher income. My own preliminary hypothesis is that once the above measures are implemented the level of BNI that will enable individuals and households to have adequate calorie intake will also be sufficient to induce them to build, or have built, for themselves adequate shelters. This is based on the observation that in 1963-64 a rural household with per capita monthly income of Tk.34 (which, as we have just argued, might be enough for an agricultural labourer to permit adequate calorie intake) apparently had reasonable housing conditions by our standards. Thus, in addition to the BNI target implied by the basic food need, the target for basic housing need may quite reasonably be set at providing land for construction and know-how for sanitary and improved design facilities.[12]

d. The Hierarchy of Basic Needs for "Private Consumption" Goods

In the above we have argued that if the basic needs for food are satisfied then those for clothing and shelter will also be satisfied. Admittedly, our estimates are illustrative and a more careful collection of facts may disprove this ordering.

Indeed, it would be very odd to find that the BNI associated with the basic need target for food is much above the BNI associated with the basic clothing need. This would go against the widely held notion that food is the primary need for poor people. More importantly, this would mean that the planner's targets of various items of basic needs are inconsistent with the people's own targets.

---

[12] An example of this is the supply of water-sealed slabs by the Public Health Engineering Department for excreta disposal in ten _thanas_ on pilot basis. This is just an example. The appropriate technology must consider cost and determine feasibility on such considerations.

There are two ways one might resolve such an inconsistency. The first is to argue that since the BNI levels corresponding to different items vary widely it must be concluded that the planner's targets are inconsistent with those of the individuals and households. One possibility then is for the planner to revise his targets. The logical way to do so would be to estimate the target for the "most important" item (e.g., food), estimate the corresponding BNI and work back to the implied basic needs levels for the other items.

Another possibility is for the planner to insist that private targets are inconsistent with social needs in so far as there may be some items in the list of "private consumption" goods which provide significant positive externalities. The logical procedure would then be to exclude such items from the list of private consumption goods and adopt policies to ensure their greater absorption through other means (e.g., public distribution and altering relative prices). In the above this is what we have suggested for certain elements of housing. To try to operate through BNI would be an inappropriate policy to ensure adequate absorption of items such as sanitation.

One final point may usefully be raised before concluding the section. To satisfy the rather elementary basic food need it will be necessary to raise the BNI for the low income groups dramatically. This would require rapid over-all growth of the economy. But the highest conceivable rate of growth will not enable such an objective to be achieved within the next decade or two. To illustrate, in 1963-64, the 40th percentile of population in the income scale from below had a per capita calorie intake of 1,935 per day. To raise the consumption of this person to 2,500 calories will require a sharp increase in income. Even if preference shifts sharply (as compared to the cross section preference) in favour of food, income will have to go up substantially. In the unlikely event of the income elasticity of calories being as high as 2/3 the annual rate of growth in per capita income will have to be nearly 4 per cent (since calorie intake will have to go up by 2.6 per cent per year if the target is to be achieved in a decade). This will imply an unprecedented rate of 6.5 per cent annual growth (even if population grows as little as 2.5 per cent per year). Even after a decade of such unprecedented growth about 40 per cent of the population will still be below the basic need target for food.

Thus a massive redistribution is in order. Such redistribution cannot be brought about by changes at the margin. Existing income earning assets will have to be redistributed. For the overwhelmingly land dependent and rural Bangladesh this underlines the absolute necessity of a thorough and equitable land redistribution programme as the precondition for the successful implementation of basic needs.

VI. The "Externality Providing" Goods and Services

a. Health

Frequently the basic need for health service is specified as a target number of medical visits per person per year. This does not appear to be a particularly helpful approach without some idea of the quality and type of service to be made available at the visit and the kind of circumstances that give rise to the need for such a visit. Before we begin a discussion of issues involved in quantifying basic health needs we want to emphasise the interrelationship among various items. Once the need for food, shelter, clothing and drinking water is satisfactorily met, the expectation of life, the rate of infant mortality and the incidence of disease will change substantially. Indeed, the implementation of a basic needs programme in other areas seems to be a necessary and perhaps very nearly a sufficient condition for a successful preventive health programme.

The first type of basic health need that the society must guarantee is the eradication of epidemics and mass disease. More concretely, this means (i) the preservation of the gain made by the eradication of small pox at the end of 1975 and the control of (ii) malaria, (iii) tuberculosis, (iv) cholera and (v) other gastro-intestinal diseases. The point to note, however, is that their eradication is almost certainly less of a medical problem and more of a social and environmental problem.

The next basic need target in health should be to provide
feasible but adequate attention in case of (i) illness;
(ii) childbirth and (iii) infant care. How can one set a
meaningful target for such services? One way to do so is to
specify a minimum target ratio of medical worker to population.
To set such a target the society must carefully balance its
health priorities against available resources in the context
of competing demands.

Today medical density (defined as the number of doctors
per population) in Bangladesh is about the lowest in the
whole world. In Africa as a whole such density is about 1.4
per 10,000 people, in Asia just under 3 and in Latin America
6.5. At the other extreme, countries with the greatest
densities are Israel (25) and the USSR (24). In Bangladesh
the density is only 0.93 per 10,000 people.[13]

A very minimum target would be to aim at achieving the
Asian average over the next 10 years or so. That will mean
one doctor for every 3.3 thousand people (i.e., approximately
550 families). But distribution can never be exactly uniform
over the whole nation. Thus with such a density there will
almost certainly be poorer rural communities where there will
be no more than one doctor for every 7 or 8 hundred families.
This is clearly inadequate.

But even this woefully inadequate target implies that the
number of doctors will have to increase by 4.5 times over the
next decade. The production of such a vast number of doctors,
quite apart from the problem of getting them to work in the
rural areas against the competition of the cities and the
medical needs of the developed western countries, will be an
impossible target.[14]

---

[13] The Bangladesh figure is from the First Five-Year Plan
(p. 500). The other figures are from Alexander Dorozynski,
Doctors and Healers, IDRC, Ottawa, 1975, p. 9.

[14] Although the medical density in Bangladesh is about the
lowest in the world it has been exporting large numbers of
doctors overseas. The same has been happening from other Asian
countries. The distribution of international income is such
that the poor people of these countries cannot compete with
the rich westerners (and more recently the oil rich sheikhdoms)
in bidding for the services of the doctors that their own
medical institutions produce.

The conclusion seems inevitable that to satisfy minimum health needs one must scrap the notion of conventional medical doctors and opt for the idea "that non-medical healers can be of tremendous service in a country where the wester-style medical doctor does not correspond to economic or cultural realities. It may be a hundred times less costly to train a healer, auxiliary, or barefoot doctor than it is to train a medical graduate. If the medical doctor leaves his country or remains in the city to compete with other medical doctors, while the health worker remains where he is needed, the cost accounting of health care delivery becomes overwhelmingly favourable to health workers. And if a medical doctor can supervise, and collaborate with, health workers strategically spread out through a large area, his effectiveness is considerably increased."[15]

It is only in the above context of widespread institutional change that it is feasible to set up reasonable targets for basic health need. It should be possible to aim at something like the target of one medical worker per 1,200 people (200 families) over the next ten to fifteen years once such changes are possible.

b. <u>Education</u>

In quantitative terms two educational targets are fairly obvious: (i) literacy for everybody; and (ii) a basic primary education for children. Literacy is a basic human need. It is the key to all cultural and recreational activities. Quite apart from favourable production effects its value as an item of consumption is very great. The task is a massive one in Bangladesh in view of the fact that approximately 80 per cent of the people are illiterate even when literacy is defined as the ability to read a simple and short sentence in Bengali. Even more than the provision of basic medical service the target of universal literacy within the next 10 to 15 years will have to depend on unconventional means of mobilising the resources at the local level and releasing the communities' latent energy.

---

[15] Alexander Dorozynski, <u>op. cit</u>. p. 55.

It is unthinkable that the Government can achieve the target in conventional ways by setting up adult literacy centres manned by teachers paid at market rate.

The primary education currently has an enrolment of 58 per cent of the 6 to 10 year age group. To raise it to 100 per cent in the next 10 to 15 years will also require fundamental change in the system. It is desirable to examine if the basic compulsory primary education should not be limited to a shorter period of say three years.

Perhaps the most important aspect of the educational programme is the question of the relevance of the content. For the people to want literacy and primary education the contents of such programmes must relate to their need. Literacy and primary education must serve as useful tools for the peasantry of Bangladesh in their understanding of the social environment and in their struggle to organise themselves to overcome their poverty and backwardness. Today the contents of such programmes in Bangladesh, as a mere glance at the textbooks will make clear, depict a world of near fantasy, a world which is completely divorced from the life of those who are meant to be educated.

c. <u>Drinking Water</u>

This is a fairly straightforward subject and a target can be set without too much difficulty. It should also be possible to implement such a programme by simple Government action at reasonable cost. Except in major urban areas drinking water must be supplied by installing tubewells. At present there are about 185 thousand tubewells in the country under Public Health Engineering Department. Allowing for the privately owned tubewells and the offsetting factor of the choking up of a sizeable proportion it is reasonable to estimate that there is one tubewell for every 70 families or so. However, this is the national average. In many communities of 100 or more families there may not exist any tubewell at all. To assure every family of having a daily use of approximately 45 minutes of a tubewell it will be necessary to provide one tubewell for every 20 families. Something like this should be the target to be implemented by the Government over the next decade or so.

d. Access to Contraception

It is not my intention to discuss the supply of contraceptive services. There is tremendous enthusiasm on the part of the Government and the donors abroad for the expansion of such services. All I would like to emphasise is that in order to ensure cost effectiveness of such a programme the planners must once again be guided by such considerations as discussed under health services. At the Gono Shastha Kendra (People's Health Centre) at Savar it has been amply demonstrated that operations such as tubal ligation can be performed by women without any medical background trained over a short period of a few months.

Here my major preoccupation is to define the basic need of a woman to have freedom from unwanted pregnancy. Such need consists of (i) the knowledge of contraception and (ii) full freedom to choose any form of contraception including abortion provided by the society at a low cost to the individual. It can easily be seen that such freedom is inextricably bound up with the broader question of the status of women. Indeed, this particular basic need is best seen as a proxy for the improved status of women.

While the formulation of a full programme for the achievement of this basic need requires a great deal of preliminary work a beginning may be made by: (i) legalising abortion and making it (as well as the other forms of contraception) available to all at low cost; (ii) abolishing inheritance and family laws that discriminate against women and (iii) ending all other economic and social discrimination against women.

VII. Some Final Comments

Let us briefly recapitulate. We started with a list of basic needs items divided into two categories:

(a) the "personal consumption" items and

(b) the other items that we put under the heading of "externality providing" goods and services.

The only reasonable approach to plan appropriate absorption of the "personal consumption" items is to provide the consumers with the necessary personal income once social intervention, in the form of influencing relative prices, gearing public distribution and similar other measures, has been optimally made. Thus the problem is to estimate the basic need levels of the consumption of such items and to determine the basic needs income level (BNI) that would permit their absorption. If the basic need levels of different items of "personal consumption" are estimated from independent considerations and not from a consideration of what will be consistent from the standpoint of the preference of the consumers then different levels of BNI will be predicted. In such an event the BNI should be estimated on the basis of the target for the item about which we feel more objective and confident (e.g., food) and work back the basic need levels of the other items. If, however, we have strong reasons to feel that the basic need level for some of these other items should be higher than the levels thus determined we should invoke policies other than raising BNI.

For the second category of goods the BNI will not be an effective instrument of ensuring appropriate consumption. The society should devise more direct methods of ensuring their adequate production and consumption although it is by no means suggested that individual consumers will not have to pay for them, partly or wholly, out of their personal incomes. The basic need targets for such items must be set by the planners on the basis of a careful balancing of priorities and resources.

Our exercise for Bangladesh is largely illustrative. Yet we are left in no doubt that a successful implementation of even a modest basic need programme would require a big effort. To achieve anything like the estimated BNI that would ensure an adequate intake of food a massive redistribution will have to take place even if the economy grows substantially.

Even after such growth and redistribution it will remain for the society to reorganise itself along quite unconventional lines to ensure the supply of basic needs like health and education. This would undoubtedly call for the mobilisation of all available resources. A precondition of such mobilisation is the abolition of the laws and institutions which act as constraints on the use of latent human energy and creativity. Above all the full participation of the people will have to be guaranteed by the unhindered institution of democracy at the grass roots.

We have not included a selection of the so-called non-material elements (e.g., basic human rights, and popular participation) in our list of basic needs. "If some statements about 'human rights' or participation are tagged onto a list of material basic needs such as food and shelter, it could carry several undesirable implications. Ethical absolutes like 'freedom' are treated in the same way as a commodity, thereby giving the impression that it is something to be dispensed at the discretion of a government. Furthermore, this 'commodity analogy' implies separability between material and non-material needs which is false. The satisfaction of material basic needs is not an end in itself and, therefore, not separable from how these needs are satisfied."[16] Democracy and popular participation, for example, are best seen as the most efficient means of achieving the basic needs targets. "This would be especially true for community services such as health and education. Innovative ways of meeting these needs through popular participation are likely to ensure greater efficiency, to provide a product more closely related to the needs of the people and also to satisfy, through the production process itself, the goal of popular involvement. It is essential, therefore, that the discussion of basic needs targets in this field should not give the impression that existing systems are the only viable ones and that meeting basic needs necessarily requires 'more of the same'."[17]

---

[16] See chapter III of this volume.

[17] Ibid.

CHAPTER V

Production Planning for Basic Needs
by
A. R. Khan

The identification and quantification of basic needs are only the first steps in the process of planning for their satisfaction. Once the target bundle of basic needs goods and services is determined the planners must face the bigger question of how to implement these targets. The two important aspects of the process of implementation are: (a) to generate and distribute income in a way that effective demand is created for the basic needs bundle of goods and services and (b) to organise production in such a way as to match demand generated by the basic needs strategy. Indeed, the generation of income and the planning of production are very closely related; the technique of production and the composition of products have important effects on the volume and distribution of income and the distribution of income powerfully affects the composition of goods produced. Also the basic needs targets themselves cannot be realistically determined without reference to the feasible structure of production and the volume and distribution of income. The ideal framework is thus a general equilibrium one in which all these inter-dependences are explicitly spelled out. What we shall try to do in the present paper is to analyse some of the crucial links in such a framework.

First, we shall try to outline the various steps involved in translating a given basic need target into a vector of aggregate consumption demand. Next, we shall analyse some of the major problems of consistency in organising production in a way that the estimated aggregate consumption demand can be satisfied with the available resources and the process of production generates and distributes income in a way that effective demand is created for the estimated vector of consumption goods. To analyse these issues we shall use, in an illustrative way, a simple multi-sector, material balance model of the type that is in widespread use in development planning. It is not our intention to recommend the use of any specific model but to show that in the usual production plans based on such models some of the vitally important links are totally neglected (thereby rendering the targets inconsistent with the feasible pattern of income distribution and resource availability) and that the usual options with respect to the production structure do not allow for the full ex-ante possibility of promoting technical flexibility through appropriate institutional changes. We shall conclude with some discussions on the decentralisation of production planning and the relevance of "comparative advantage" as a principle guiding the organisation of production.

The issues discussed in this paper are well known and no originality is being claimed for the solutions suggested. Indeed many of the related issues have been analysed by others, sometimes in great detail.[1] All the present paper tries to do is to focus sharply on the various problems of feasibility that a basic needs plan will run into unless the close interrelation among the basic needs targets, the production structure and the distribution of income is incorporated into such a plan.

I. Estimating Consumption Demand

At the risk of appearing to be labouring an obvious point it is necessary to begin by dispelling the notion that multiplying the per capita basic needs target (or targets) of a given commodity by total population (or the numbers of people relevant for different targets) would provide a useful estimate of the consumption demand for that commodity.[2] This is

---

[1] See Hopkins, Scolnik and McLean, "Basic Needs, Growth and Redistribution: A Quantitative Approach" in ILO, <u>Tripartite World Conference on Employment, Income Distribution and Social Progress and the International Division of Labour, Background Papers, Volume I</u>, Geneva 1976; Hopkins, Rodgers and Wéry, "Evaluating a Basic Needs Strategy and Population Policies: the BACHUE Approach", in <u>International Labour Review</u>, November-December 1976 and the various references in these two papers.

[2] The discussion at this stage is on the method of estimating the aggregate consumption demand of the private consumption goods. See the classification introduced in Chapter IV.

because of the simple fact that the personal income of every
individual or household would not be exactly the same as the
basic needs income. Even if it is possible to ensure that no
one is left below the basic need income some (perhaps considerable)
inequality in the distribution of income above the basic need
level will inevitably remain. As a consequence more (or less
if the commodity in question is an "inferior good" in the sense
of being subject to a negative income elasticity of demand)
than the basic need target of a commodity would be demanded by
those with higher than basic need income. If total supply is
merely capable of ensuring overall per capita consumption at the
level of the basic need target then the inequality in the distribution of income would lead to an unequal distribution of the
commodity with the consequence that for some the basic need
target would not be achieved. Thus, in order to ensure adequate
supply to satisfy basic needs one must allow also for the extra
demand that is likely to be generated by those with higher
incomes.[3]

Let us illustrate the various steps involved in the process
of estimating the demand for private consumption goods and
services. The overall income target for the society must be
broken down into incomes of the different classes for the major
ecological areas (e.g., urban and rural).[4] To do so the
minimum feasible inequality in the distribution of income has to
be predicted on the basis of a careful evaluation of the possibilities with respect to such factors as the redistribution of

---

[3] It may be suggested that the problem can be resolved
by distribution control. Such control may be resorted to temporarily or for an extended period in case of a few special items.
But complete distribution control means that income distribution
would be fully determined by the rationing of the consumption
goods. Apart from the massive administrative input involved in
such a programme it is an inefficient device to redistribute
income.

[4] For simplicity we are assuming that the planning exercise
will start from some target income and try to minimise the cost
of achieving the target in terms of resources. It is possible
that the planners would want to reverse the sequence by starting
from a given bundle of resources and trying to plan for maximum income. In the latter case the group incomes would be derived
endogenously from the general equilibrium framework.

income-producing assets (e.g. land), the flexibility of the structure and technique of production and the limits of direct income redistributive measures at the disposal of the planners in the context of the constraints arising out of the need to provide adequate incentives. Once some broad idea is formed about the degree of minimum feasible inequality it should be possible to divide the overall income target into incomes of the different classes of people in the different ecological areas. The next step is to use the estimated consumption function[5] for each group to predict demand. The sum of such predicted demands would give the aggregate consumption demand that must be balanced by supply obtained from domestic production and net imports. Unless the commodity in question is an "inferior good" the total demand thus estimated would be greater than the basic need target multiplied by population.

As we have discussed in Chapter IV, the targets for the "externality producing" items (e.g. health and education) have to be set on the basis of criteria which are very different from those that determine the targets for personal consumption goods and services. However, one must take into account the possibility that there will continue to be a private (albeit a limited one) market for such services. To the extent it is possible for higher income people to buy health and education it would be necessary to allow for their likely purchases, over and above the basic need targets, in estimating total demand.

II. The Planning of Production

It is not our purpose in this paper to try to develop a complete model of production planning for the satisfaction of basic needs. Instead, we shall try to identify those linkages

---

[5]The consumption patterns revealed by the household expenditure surveys would have to serve as the main basis for the estimation of these functions but caution must be exercised in allowing for changes in income distribution that are followed by expected changes in preference only with a time lag. Thus, a drastic land reform may raise the income level of the recently landless to the level of the small or medium peasants. But it would be wrong to expect an instantaneous adjustment of their consumption pattern to that of the small or medium peasants.

in a production plan that play a vitally important role in determining the feasibility of a basic need target. In doing so we should also be able to identify the links in the production process with respect to which we have some degrees of freedom in ensuring the feasibility of a basic need target.

To avoid talking in the abstract we shall outline a somewhat stylised version of the kind of material balance models for production planning that have been widely used in the developing countries. We shall neglect many realistic aspects of an economy just to keep the description of the basic working of the model simple. Let the economy be divided into a number of homogeneous sectors. The supply demand balance for the product of sector i in the target year would be as follows (for notation see the table on the next page).

(1) $X_i + M_i = \sum_j X_{ij} + \sum_j B_{ij} + C_i + G_i + E_i$

In such a material balance model it is usual to make the various elements endogenous by postulating technological inter-relationships.[6] Thus the current input flows, the X_{ij}s, would be related to the level of output of the using sectors by way of the standard Leontief coefficients:

(2) $X_{ij} = a_{ij} X_j$

In making the capital input flows, the B_{ij}s, endogenous let us first consider total investment required to be undertaken between the beginning (year 1) and the end (the target year T) of the plan period:

(3) $\sum_{t=1}^{T} B_{ij}^t = b_{ij} (X_j^{T+\Theta} - \bar{X}_j)$

---

[6] The specific inter-relationships postulated in the current exposition are largely illustrative and we do not make the claim that they are the most accurate or realistic ones.

Investment is related to the volume of additional capacity creation by way of the fixed incremental capital coefficients, b_{ij}. It is assumed that investment undertaken during the plan period will, on the average, contribute to capacity creation θ years after the application of the capital input.

Table of Notations

Subscripts (i,j) denote sectors. Double subscripts (ij) mean delivery from sector i to sector j. Unsuperscripted variables denote values in the terminal year of the plan. Otherwise superscripts refer to time periods.

Variables

Y = sectoral output

$\bar{X}$ = "benchmark" output capacity (i.e., output in the immediate pre-plan year plus capacity in the pipeline due to investment undertaken before the start of the plan)

X_{ij} = intersectoral current input delivery

B_{ij} = intersectoral capital input delivery

C = household (private) consumption

G = public consumption, including the publicly provided items of private consumption

E = export

M = import (prefixes a, b and c representing imports of "maintenance", capital and consumption goods)

Parameters

a_{ij} = current input coefficients

b_{ij} = incremental capital coefficients

θ = average investment output lag

g = rate of growth of investment

q = post terminal sectoral growth rate

m_{ij} = maintenance import of the i-th good required per unit of output in sector j

u_i = proportion of the i-th capital good that has to be obtained from imports

r_i = consumption import as proportion of consumption demand

t = time period ($t = 0$ is the immediate pre-plan year; $t = T$ is the terminal year of the plan, etc.)

The incremental capacity requirement is defined to be the difference between the demand for output Θ years after the target year and the "benchmark output" which consists of the capacity available in the immediate pre-plan year plus the additional capacity in the pipeline that would result from the investment wholly undertaken during the pre-plan period.

In the balance equation (1) only the investment in the target year is shown while in equation (3) the total investment over the entire plan is shown. To obtain the former from the latter we would postulate a time path of investment between year 1 and T. If we assume that investment is so scheduled that it grows in a sector at the annual compound rate of g then we can define:

$$(4) \quad h = \frac{B_{ij}}{\sum_{t=1}^{T} B_{ij}^{t}} = \frac{(1+g)^T B_{ij}^o}{\sum_{t=1}^{T}(1+g)^t B_{ij}^o} = \frac{(1+g)^T}{\sum_{t=1}^{T}(1+g)^t}$$

To eliminate the sectoral outputs for a post-terminal year from the balance equation (1) let us also postulate post-terminal rates of growth for the various sectors:

$$(5) \quad X_j^{T+\Theta} = (1+q)^{\Theta} X_j$$

By combining (3), (4) and (5) we can now have the following expression for investment in the terminal year (making allowance for the non-negativity of investment even in the unlikely case of declining sectoral capacity requirement):

$$(6) \quad B_{ij} = h\, b_{ij} [(1+q)^{\Theta} X_j - \bar{X}_j] \text{ if } X_j > \bar{X}_j$$
$$\qquad = 0 \text{ if } X_j \leq \bar{X}_j$$

Imports are usually divided into the imports of current inputs ($_aM_i$), capital goods ($_bM_i$) and consumption goods ($_cM_i$) and the levels of these components can be postulated to be determined as follows:

(7a) $\quad _aM_i = \sum_j m_{ij} x_j$

(7b) $\quad _bM_i = u_i \sum_j B_{ij}$

(7c) $\quad _cM_i = r_i (C_i + G_i)$

Substituting (2), and (6) through (7c) into (1) we get the final form of the balance equations:[7]

(8)
$$X_i - \sum_j (a_{ij} - m_{ij}) X_j - (1 - u_i) h \sum_j b_{ij} [(1 + q)^\theta X_j - \bar{X}_j]$$
$$= (1 - r_i)(C_i + G_i) + E_i$$

Assuming that feasible limits to exports are determined independently a plan in this framework consists of setting targets with respect to consumption, both private and public. In the earlier part of this paper we discussed how one could estimate the vectors of private and public consumption demand to satisfy the basic need criteria. Could we then say that production planning to satisfy basic needs simply consists of the following steps: (i) estimating the target vectors of C and G, (ii) making estimates of the parameters like a_{ij}, m_{ij} and u_i on the basis of the existing or some feasible alternative patterns of technology and trade, (iii) solving the system of equations (8) and (iv) determining the requirement of resources (capital and foreign exchange) by using the investment and import equations? We shall show in the following sections why such a simple procedure will prove inadequate.

---

[7] As already stated this is an oversimplified version of the usual kind of material balance models applied in some developing countries. Demands for working capital and replacement have not been separately shown. Various assumptions with respect to lag, time path of investment, etc., are oversimplified. In an actual planning model more details are usually shown and the various inter-relationships specified with greater care and attention to reality.

III. Some Problems of Consistency

We shall consider two types of problems of consistency that are left out of the pure material balance approach adopted in the above type of planning framework. The first is the consistency between income generation and effective consumption demand. The process of income generation has not been made endogenous in the above framework. For each sector the value added $(P_j X_j - \sum_i P_i a_{ij} X_j$ where P_i = price of the i-th product) is distributed in some way among the different categories of the owners of primary factors of production (e.g., labour, land and capital). The distribution of such income among various classes and income groups must be such that, given the further redistribution that might be feasible through fiscal policy, the basic needs bundle of consumption goods would be demanded by everybody.[8] The composition of goods and the range of techniques must be flexible enough to provide employment to such numbers at such wages that the redistributive public policy is able to bear the residual burden.[9]

---

[8] A qualification is in order. For those just around the level of basic need income the commodity composition of the basic need target can be determined by following the methodology outlined in Chapter IV. There is no need for everyone to be above this particular commodity bundle corresponding to the basic needs. A richer family would probably satisfy its energy requirements by consuming wheat whereas the poorer ones would conform to the cheaper bundle that would include millet.

[9] For example, the Draft Fifth Five-Year Plan of India and the First Five-Year Plan of Bangladesh both had the objective of satisfying some of the minimum physical needs of the people. On that basis these plans drew up aggregate consumption targets. Both the plans used multisectoral frames of the type illustrated above to derive production and investment plans. Both the plans remained unconvincing on the question of the consistency between the distribution of income and the target consumption. While a great deal of pious wish was expressed to that end, none of the plans demonstrated that the production plan would provide a distribution of income that would create effective demand for the target bundle of consumption goods in such a way that few would remain below the minimum needs.

It must be recognised that in a typical developing society it is impossible to provide any significant proportion of the population with unemployment benefit and/or wage supplement. Thus the feasibility of the basic needs consumption targets (C_i and G_i in equations 8) would depend on the employment (or self employment) of enough earners per household at a high enough wage (or income). If sufficient information is available on the employment of the different types of workers at different wages in each sector, the dependency ratios for various types of workers, and so on, then the above material balance model could be extended to determine the feasibility, or otherwise, of the basic need consumption target.

What must be recognised is that in any given institutional organisation of the economy it may be impossible to employ the necessary numbers at high enough wages to ensure effective demand for basic need consumption bundle.[10] Thus, in a densely populated rural economy with highly skewed distribution of land ownership the only feasible wage rate at which sufficient numbers may be employed would probably be way below what would be necessary

---

[10] Thus consider the following distribution of value added among the primary factors of production:

$$P_j X_j = \sum_i P_i a_{ij} X_j + \sum_i w_i l_{ij} X_j + K_j$$

where l_{ij} = man years of i-th class of workers required per unit of j

w_i = wage rate for the i-th class of workers

K_j = profit in sector j (the residual).

The income per earner of the i-th class will be

$$(w_i \sum_j l_{ij} X_j) / N_i,$$

where N_i = the number of labourers belonging to the i-th class, and per capita income in an average family of the i-th class of workers will be

$$(w_i \sum_j l_{ij} X_j / N_i D_i)$$

where D_i = the number of dependants per employed worker in the the i-th class. There is no guarantee that this amount would be above the basic need income. More importantly, this is just the average income for the i-th class of workers. There will be considerable variation within the class if only the dependency ratio would differ between households.

to create demand for the basic need consumption bundle. In such a situation the feasibility of the basic need target would crucially depend on the ability of the society to change the institutional framework within which production activities are carried out.

The second type of consistency that the planners must try to ensure is that between the requirement and availability of resources. The solution of the system of equations (8) would indicate a level of investment requirement that may be far in excess of the capacity of the society to save, given the level and distribution of income. Also, the level of import requirement may exceed the export earnings by a very wide margin.[11] In either case there would be a requirement of very large inflow of foreign capital which would either not be forthcoming or be inconsistent with the minimum degree of self-reliance that is a necessary condition of the long-term success of a basic need strategy.[12]

To avoid this type of inconsistency it is necessary that the technical coefficients and the behavioural relations of the system are flexible within a sufficiently wide range. Let us illustrate some of the available degrees of freedom:

---

[11] Ex post, the two gaps would be equal.

[12] The definition of minimum self-reliance is by no means easy. But several criteria are obvious. First, one must consider the question of feasibility. The planners must not recommend a production plan which entails a foreign exchange gap that is bigger than the available capital inflow. Secondly, even if loans were available, the planners must consider whether the repayment burden in future would become too large to allow the country to continue to make progress along the basic need oriented development path. Finally, the level of foreign borrowing and the inflow of direct foreign investment must not be allowed to commit the technology of the country to what is available in the donor countries irrespective of the question of appropriateness.

(a) It would usually be possible to satisfy a given basic need with alternative goods. Thus a given amount of calorie can be provided by different items of food that require different amounts of scarce resources. Clothing requirement can be met by the products of handloom or those of large mechanised weaving mills. It would make sense to price goods and services in a way that resource costs are proportionately reflected so that in the basic need targets (C_i in equation 8) private households arrive at a lower weight for the goods and services that use scarce resources intensively.

(b) There would usually be a number of alternative ways of producing a particular good. Once a commodity is chosen the degree of freedom with respect to the current input coefficients (the a_{ij}s) would be limited (the cotton or yarn component of a metre of textile is roughly the same irrespective of whether the latter is produced by handlooms or in mechanised mills). But the choice with respect to the capital coefficients (the b_{ij}s) and the foreign exchange coefficients (particularly the u_is) would be quite large. Thus the system of incentives should be organised in a way that maximum advantage of such flexibility is taken by those who decide what may be called the techniques in a broad sense.

However, it is quite possible that, given the social institutions, some highly desirable technological alternatives would remain irrelevant from an operational standpoint. An example may be found in the possible fishery development in the derelict tanks in a country like Bangladesh. It has frequently been pointed out that in such a protein-starved society the development of the derelict tanks could bring about qualitative improvement in the standard of diet. It has also been recognised that the socially cheapest way of doing so is to employ the large army of unemployed labour with very rudimentary equipment. But the derelict tanks are mostly privately owned and if the owners are to develop them as private enterprise then labour has to be hired at market wage which immediately limits employment below what is socially desirable. Moreover, the owners must be able to enforce proprietary rights be erecting fences (thereby raising the b_{ij}s) or stationing guards (which increases costs). Thus the cheapest technique is irrelevant within the given social context. It would be relevant only if the availability of unemployed labour coincided with the ownership of tanks. For similar reasons the development of land through capital construction by otherwise unemployed labour is rendered impossible in a society with unequal distribution of land ownership.

To summarise our discussion above, the basic need targets can be meaningfully set only by integrating them with the structure of production and income generation. Estimating a vector of consumption goods that would satisfy the planners' criteria of what is "decent" or "minimum" conditions of human existence is by itself a meaningless exercise unless it is an integral part of a broader plan that incorporates feasible solutions to two other related issues: (a) the structure of production is such that the basic need targets can be matched by appropriate production in a reasonably self-reliant manner; and (b) the generation and distribution of income in the process of production is such that the effective demand for the basic need bundle is created with minimal burden on directly redistributive action by the Government.

The simple extrapolation of the production structure and the production relations is unlikely to satisfy these feasibility conditions in a typical underdeveloped economy.[13] Without

---

[13] By now there exists an impressive volume of empirical literature to show that the resource intensity of techniques in the developing countries is much greater than what it should be. Also, the pattern of asset ownership and the organisation of production is such that the incremental income distribution is at best no better than the average distribution. Both the actual planning experience and demonstration planning exercise in a number of developing countries show that the attempt to grow at a high enough rate tends to bring about too large a resource gap and exacerbate the inequality in the distribution of income.

doubt some improvement could be brought about by adopting the standard policies (e.g. removing distortions in relative factor prices) that encourage the movement towards more appropriate techniques of production. But in a situation of massive unemployment and extreme poverty such micro adjustments will usually be inadequate to promote the kind of product composition and technology of production that would provide enough incomes to sufficient numbers. What would be necessary is to broaden the range of feasible techniques by breaking the institutional barriers and to lower the cost of producing a unit of composite output by directing demand to goods and services that are cheaper to produce.

It has been argued that these factors reinforce each other to lead to a convergence to the final objective. A more egalitarian distribution of income, it is claimed, leads to a composition of consumption which is cheaper to produce in terms of scarce inputs (capital and foreign exchange). Such a commodity basket is believed to represent much greater labour intensity than does a basket that would be demanded if the distribution of income were less equal. A greater degree of labour-intensity in the technique of production is likely to promote greater equality in the distribution of income. For every single case the validity of the above claims will have to be ascertained. Only by trying to push each of the above degrees of freedom to its optimum limit can a poor society hope to satisfy the basic human needs of its population within a reasonable time horizon.

IV. Decentralised Production Planning

The above discussion should not create the impression that in our view the best way to plan for the satisfaction of basic need is for the central planners to estimate the target vector of basic need consumption bundle, plan the appropriate composition of goods and determine the appropriate technique of production from a global standpoint. There is little hope that such central direction would promote the kind of ingenuity that is necessary to exploit the full advantage of the available degrees of freedom which are relatively few in number.

To allow the mobilisation of unemployed labour along unconventional lines it is essential to ensure full participation of the masses. Planning must largely become decentralised to the extent of allowing the local communities to set up their own targets and to plan production and distribution to achieve those targets. It is beyond the capacity of the wisest central planning organisation to devise ingenuous methods of mobilising unused resources at different local levels that differ widely with respect to local circumstances. Much more than in an advanced industrial society planning for the removal of poverty in a poor society, requiring unorthodox methods, must be decentralised.

What then is the relevance of the global exercise that we discussed above? If local communities are to set up their own targets then what possible use do the global targets have? If techniques and production structures have to be devised at the local level then what role does global planning have to perform?

The global exercise is still of crucial relevance in many ways. The central authority must provide a macro-economic context within which decentralised planning can take place. It will be beyond the capacity of the local community to remove the institutional barriers to local mobilisation on their own. The global planners and the central authorities must provide assistance and decisive support in this regard. A good many other actions must be centrally organised. To this category belongs the task of setting the appropriate price relationships, organising activities that are subject to important economies of scale, maintaining the supply demand balance for non-local inputs and selectively providing skills, resources and information where necessary. To perform these functions effectively the global planners must carry out a global exercise to understand the magnitude of the problem, identify the institutional barriers and obtain guidelines for its own actions.

Such global planning can be successfully carried out only if there is constant interaction between the global and local planners. Thus, for example, the global targets must be based and revised on the basis of continuous evaluation of the local targets. A prosperous local community will set its own basic need targets above the level of that set by a poor community. In this situation the notion of the uniform application of some global basic need targets to every local community would have little relevance. Nor would it be of much use to argue that the same global basic need standards must be enforced everywhere by effective transfers from the richer to the poorer communities. As the experience of China has amply demonstrated such transfers cannot be of significantly large magnitude without seriously impairing local incentives both for the donors and the recipients.

V. Comparative Advantage and Basic Needs

To what extent must the basic need bundle of goods and services be produced by the local community that would consume it? Should such communities be developed as self-sufficient and relatively autarkic entities?

It would appear to be wholly unnecessary to deprive the poor communities of the advantage of specialisation if such advantage is real and in excess of the offsetting costs of transport, uncertainty and such other elements. It is the task of the global planner to keep the price relations proportional to costs to the society so that the local communities can perceive the advantage of specialisation and trade. The global planners could go further and provide the intermediation in exchange between the local communities.

The proponents of self-sufficient rural communities argue that trade between such communities in a poor society is in fact very small. From this observation they conclude that it is unrealistic to expect that trade will develop among such communities even when they begin to advance along the path towards the basic need targets.

The reason trade is observed to be virtually non-existent between poor rural communities within the third world countries is largely the lack of demand. Growth is concentrated in the urban areas which generate demand that pulls food and other "surplus" out of the rural communities. Another part responds to the pull of demand from abroad. Other rural communities, stagnating in poverty, cannot compete with urban and foreign demand to bid away goods from the fellow rural communities.

There is no need for this pattern to continue to obtain once basic need oriented growth takes place. Supply in one community will create demand for the other communities in what would amount to the fulfilment of Say's law. Moreover, a good deal of the basic need consumption demand in such local communities would consist of goods (e.g. earthenware pots and pans, rudimentary furnitures, housing made of indigenous materials, local dress and so on) which require little fixed capital to produce. Thus, in such cases, demand will create its own supply.

What seems to be a reasonable policy for individual communities to follow also appears to be useful guidelines for action by individual countries. If basic need targets can be achieved with less aggregate resources by allowing the country to produce certain goods for exports with which to buy from abroad some items in the basic need bundle then it would clearly be desirable to do so. The most convincing case for such national specialisation and trade is illustrated by the fact that such exchange between two developing nations can only quicken the pace of their advance towards their basic need targets.

Some proponents of national autarky argue that trade on the basis of "comparative advantage" is harmful to the basic need strategy in so far as such trade influences personal consumption to be oriented towards luxury imports and limits production techniques to the ones that can be imported from the technologically advanced countries. If these dangers are real then appropriate adjustments must be made in the "comparative advantage" calculations. If adhering to the comparative advantage calculations on the basis of the available techniques makes it impossible to evolve appropriate techniques that are currently unavailable then one must think in terms of a broader infant industry criterion that protects unborn infants as well.[14]

It is important to realise that the argument is not that comparative advantage calculations should be based on the assumption of the optimality of free trade. Such calculations should be based on the criterion of maximising the basic needs objectives from available resources. If specialisation and exchange leads to the attainment of a higher level of basic need from given resources then it is misplaced heroism to condemn the nation to autarky.

---

[14] The argument that potential import of luxury goods would create pressure for greater inequality in the distribution of income seems to be less convincing. Potentially luxury goods can also be produced domestically and the shutting out of imports is no guarantee that the pressure for luxury consumption and consequent inequality would be reduced.

www.ingramcontent.com/pod-product-compliance
Ingram Content Group UK Ltd.
Pitfield, Milton Keynes, MK11 3LW, UK
UKHW021321180426
11947UKWH00015B/1364